ON AMERICA'S ROADS

To Jakeyah,

Even though I have
not told you, you are
an inspiration to Me!

Thank You for your
support.

2/29/19

ON AMERICA'S ROADS

SOMEONE'S LIFE DEPENDS UPON YOUR OBEDIENCE

JERMAINE A. AARON

TATE PUBLISHING & *Enterprises*

Published by Tate Publishing & Enterprises, LLC
127 E. Trade Center Terrace | Mustang, Oklahoma 73064 USA
1.888.361.9473 | www.tatepublishing.com

Tate Publishing is committed to excellence in the publishing industry. The company reflects the philosophy established by the founders, based on Psalm 68:11,
"The Lord gave the word and great was the company of those who published it."

Book design copyright © 2008 by Tate Publishing, LLC. All rights reserved.
Cover design by Eddie Russell
Interior design by Nathan Harmony

Published in the United States of America
ISBN: 978-1-60462-247-8
1. Nonfiction: Automotive: General/Dri
08.01.15

To the millions of families of the victims whom have perished on our roads, we want you to know that we have heard your cry, and to say that we are committed to doing what is right so that your loss shall not be in vain.

Acknowledgements

There are several individuals, agencies, and organizations that have contributed tremendously to this assignment to which I would like to say many thanks.

First, I am thankful to my Heavenly Father for infusing me with the knowledge and wisdom in bringing this assignment to completion. Father, your continual guidance both in prayer and in meditation was most remarkable. I have enjoyed your wonderful sense of humor and the detailed insight you have given to me to convey the message of driving with integrity to my fellow citizens. To you belongs all of the praise. Thank you!

To my awesome pastors, Mason and Twyla Betha, I thank you both tremendously for your prayers for all of us at S.A.N.E. Church International. Your love for me and your many encouragements have been uplifting, and have impelled me to finish my assignment. Every message I have ever heard from your mouths has empowered me to walk in love and to experience "total-life" prosperity.

Furthermore, I want to thank Dr. Frederick K.C. Price for his steadfast devotion to living a life of integrity. Dr. Price, it was your remarks on the EIFM website entitled "Rolling Stops" that has first influenced me to change my thinking and thus my attitude towards driving. Thank you very much for your commitment to excellence!

To Michelle Brown, I would like to say many thanks for your enduring commitment in holding me accountable to finishing my assignment. From the moment I made you aware of driving with integrity, you have been a true ambassador of this lifestyle. You ran with this assignment as if it was your own to begin with. I thank you for your amazing support—both spiritually and financially. I know that you are committed to seeing people's lives changed for the better. Thank you, again!

To Rodney and Tameeka Williamson, I am delighted to have you both as ambassadors of driving with integrity. Your faithfulness in doing what is right sets you beyond reproach. Thank you for holding me accountable to what I say I believe and for doing the speed limit in spite of popular belief and practice.

I am very grateful for Quentin and Likisha Stanley, Alexander and Christina McClain, Floyd Calhoun, Kimberly Bailey, Mike Edwards, Jennifer Pedraza, and Winston Riddick for their wonderful words of encouragement. Your abundant prayers of agreement and your strong conviction in what I was purposed to do have strengthened me in times of great adversities.

A special thanks to Officer M.B. Pension and the entire DeKalb County, Georgia Police Department. Your unwavering commitment to justice and peace is truly remarkable. I would like to personally thank Officer M.B. Pension for agreeing to take me on a Ride-A-Long back in April 2006. You have given me the opportunity to see firsthand what you all have to deal with on a daily basis. Thank you all for your honorable service!

In addition, I must say "Thank You" to my awesome students at Southwest DeKalb (SWD) High School. You all have really encouraged me to want to know more about teen driving. You guys are the best! I always believe in you and your abilities. Now, may you prosper in every good thing you put your minds to accomplish, and remember that, "Success is when preparation meets opportunity." Therefore, drive safe and with integrity, and enjoy your lives!

A special note of thanks to the National Highway Traffic Safety Administration (NHTSA), NHTSA National Center for Statistics and Analysis (NCSA), the Governor's Highway Safety Association (GHSA), the Virginia Department of Transportation (VDOT), the U.S. Department of Transportation (U.S. DOT), the Federal Highway Administration (FHWA), the Insurance Institute for Highway Safety (IIHS), the New York State Department of Motor Vehicle (NYS DMV), the International Association of Chiefs of Police (IACP), the Detroit News, the Chicago Tribune, the Atlanta Journal Constitution (AJC), USA Today, Fox5 News (Atlanta, GA), ABC News, and NBC News, for their continued effort in making our driving public aware of the consequences of its driving. The statistics you provide are invaluable. I am thankful for your many programs geared towards reducing motor vehicle crashes and fatalities. Your enduring service is well appreciated. Thank you all in abundance!

Table of Contents

A Note from the Author

Dear reader,

It is an honor to be given the opportunity to write to you concerning the nature of driving on America's roads. The information in this book is written with the intent to help save lives by providing ample statistics of the conditions that exist on our roads and illustrating a more excellent means of commuting on our nation's interstates, highways, and other service roads.

You will discover that most of the federal statistics referenced are from 2004 or earlier. The reason for this is when I began researching motor vehicle crashes and fatalities the latest annual federal compilation of motor vehicle crashes and fatalities was from 2004. It was not until late 2006 that the National Highway Traffic Safety Administration (NHTSA) released an early edition of its 2005 statistics, and the final version in 2007. The web address to this final version can be found in the reference section.

While there are those who support speeding and other dangerous driving habits and practices, and have written about their so-called "success" in doing so, I refrained from mentioning their names because it is not my purpose to malign anyone. However, I have summarized what some have said in order to deal with principles and not the person.

Chapter 2 contains some serious reasoning, and thus I strongly recommend that you read it with caution and in its entirety before making a value judgment. I say this because it is quite easy for some people to misinterpret what I have written in this chapter. My only intention was to illustrate why things happen. History teaches many lessons and one of them is to always learn from the past. Hence, the content of this chapter clearly shows why we see what we see and not to tread upon people's religious beliefs.

Because driving is, for many people in America, a necessity, I strongly recommend that you apply the principles of driving with integrity shared in this book to your driving and to as many people you come in contact with on a daily basis, especially with those you care about. All it takes is your willingness and obedience to do what is right. Therefore, make today count! Submit to the traffic laws by applying the principles of integrity driving to your life and share what you have learned, because your life is worth exceeding, abundantly, far more than what others see. You were born to make a positive difference!

Thank you for your cooperation in making our roads safer for all those traveling around you.

In the Service of Promoting Excellence in Driving,

Jermaine A. Aaron
Integrity Driving (ID)

Preface

Children are truly a delight and a joy. We all were once little children, born into this world as a joy to our parents and loved by many who came in contact with us. They laughed and made funny faces and baby talked us. We giggled at their remarks and funny faces, which encouraged them to continue in their joy.

Unfortunately, the lives of many of these children ended abruptly. They never made it to the end of their destiny; they were never permitted to live a fulfilled life and reach the full length of their days. They never lived their full life because it was stolen in a motor vehicle crash.

There are many organizations that sponsor children in hopes of saving their lives, to give them another shot to become great and have an abundantly satisfied life. These organizations sometimes take children off the streets who would have otherwise taken their lives either by drugs, guns, gangs, or any other detrimental means. Consider the outcome of this child's life.

> Say you decided to sponsor an adorable, beautiful, and charming little child, whether by being a parent/guardian, or by being a big brother or sister. You feel good about your decision, because

deep down, you believe you have done the right thing—you have given a child back his life, an opportunity to become somebody. Your sponsored child/sibling is showing signs of becoming great: his grades are excellent, he never gets into a fight, and he is patient, kind, and obedient in almost everything. You tell everyone you meet about your joy, and they eventually fall in love with your story.

But like the unfortunate outcome mentioned above, your joy was never meant to be. While crossing the street to go to school, this child's life was reduced to death by a driver who was in a hurry to get to where he was going and made the decision to run the red light. The people who witnessed the crash heard a loud noise and saw a child tossed about twenty feet into the air and thrown about one hundred feet from the intersection. They rushed to him, only to see him drowning in his own blood. What a loss! What a tragedy! All you can feel now is pain, anger, and misery. You have lost the love and joy of your life because someone made the decision to ignore the law. That child's life depended upon that driver's obedience!

I ask you, "How can we save another life on our roads?"

I write to you, America, because I believe you will change; I believe you will change your mindset towards driving, and doing so with integrity. I write to you, parents and adults, because you are a beacon of light to your children, an example they can and will follow. I write to you, young adults and teen drivers, because America's great destiny is in your capable hands, and its legacy will continue through you and your children. I write to you, America, because the world is watching us and is encouraged by our firmness towards righteousness and justice, towards positive change and freedom, towards peace and safety, and towards the belief that all men are created equal and that "... *when the rights of one man are denied, the rights of all men are denied*," as John F. Kennedy once said.

Introduction

(Sowing Seeds)

If you can ascertain one fact or one truth that would save your life, would you be willing to learn it and practice it? If you honestly say yes, then the information in this book will be of significant benefit to you.

> About thirteen years ago I sat in the front passenger seat of my family's white Toyota Tercel while my stepfather took me for a ride on Interstate 20. As we headed east, I noticed the speedometer gradually increased to about 65 mph on a 55 mph stretch. When I informed my stepfather that he was going beyond the speed limit, he remarked something to the effect that his foot fell asleep on him—it got heavy.

> I thought this was the norm because he had been driving for quite sometime, so he would know a thing or two about cruising at the speed limit. Little did I know a seed was planted in my mind: "It is impossible to go at the speed limit; no one has that kind of control."

Shortly after I got my license, I discovered this seed was absolutely true for someone with no self-control. Through the years, with careful and joyful watering, this seed grew to the point where I thought my life was going to end on the roads. My driving was way out of control, and as a result, it caused a transfer of hundreds of my well-earned dollars to our police departments, the details of which I will share later.

If you are known for your speeding, I am telling you today, your life is worth far more than a few minutes of illegal pleasure. This truth I wish I knew back in 2002 when the State of North Carolina hit me for a cool $350 for cruising at 80 mph in a 55 mph zone, right at the beginning of the most celebrated season of the year—Christmas! I was infuriated because I had other plans for that money. I went to the stores wishing that I had never met that officer. In fact, every thing I desired I could not buy, even though some of them cost more than the money I shelled out for the citation (plus lawyer fees). I said to myself, *Man, I'm never going to speed again!* But this was a futile promise; the next year I got another citation for repeating 80 in a 55 zone. Yes, I was like a dog that returned to its own vomit—I did not learn a thing from being punished with a $350 citation, not to mention being caught three more times within the span of a few months.

So all that pleasure really was not pleasurable because when I thought the police departments got me, I did not know their cousins (the insurance companies) also got me. One citation actually goes a very long way: a minimum of three years penalty by many insurance companies, not to mention the penalty reaped by getting two, three, or four citations.

But today life is very good because no officer of the law can morally or legally cite me for a speeding violation! And better yet, I do not need to figure out how to get out of a speeding ticket, because as a driver, I have learned and am practicing the only remedy for not getting a speeding ticket—*do not speed!* Now, there are some books on the market that teach you how to beat a speeding ticket, how to get out of a speeding ticket every time, or how to speed and not get caught. Each one I read supported the idea of speeding—just don't get caught, or if you do manage to reel in a ticket, then follow the prescribed steps of abusing the law to beat the law. I am not knocking those authors. I am, however, dealing with a principle: if you buy such a book for the sole purpose of getting out of a speeding ticket, you will end up having to repeat this process. Why? Because the one thing that was supposed to change was never dealt with—your attitude towards obeying the traffic laws.

To this end I submit to you that once you get a revelation of the magnitude of the way we drive in this country, your attitude will change and you will begin to develop a greater appreciation for the traffic laws. Remember this: moral and just laws are not an encroachment on your driving enjoyment. They exist to preserve your life so that you may live longer and enjoy the company of your loved ones, and to remind you that you are important. When the department of transportation posts a sign on the highway that says, "Slow Down, Dangerous Curve," they are not trying to steal your joy; rather they are trying to preserve your life, so the person who truly loves you may have another chance to enjoy your company; that your children may never feel the pain and agony of having their parent(s) snatched from them, never to return; that your spouse will not have to live a shattered life; that your parents may not have to live another day in tears knowing you were born to make a positive difference, but now that will never happen; and that your life does not have to end on the roads.

These are some of the things I was not conscious of years ago; I really thought I could do whatever I wanted and not have to deal with the consequences. The same can be said for many drivers today. They believe they should decide what is safe, even if it means failing to yield to what is right. Like I said, there is a gallimaufry of products that promise to show you how to beat a speeding ticket. If we all decide to ignore the speed limit by driving above it at speeds we feel comfortable, which many people do practice, then who is to say that the next life to be snuffed out will not be yours?

The days of existential thinking are still here, and we saw this way of thinking on September 11, 2001, when terrorists took their hatred and repugnance for Americans and rammed them into the World Trade Center in New York. Guess what? Those terrorists believed they were justified in what they sought out to do. Similarly, this mindset is prevalent on our roads. Speeders do not find any error in speeding, yet they do not like getting speeding tickets. In fact, no one, to my knowledge, enjoys getting a speeding ticket. Who enjoys getting hit for his well-earned dollars? Nevertheless, if you practice doing the wrong things, you will reap a corresponding effect, just like if you practice doing the right things then it will go well with you. It is called the law of sowing and reaping.

Therefore, I submit to you the only true and tested way to avoid a speeding ticket and any other traffic violation is to agree to obey the traffic laws.

The Statistics of Our Roads
(Where Are Our Fellow Americans?)

Let me ask you a few questions. How many members are in your extended family? How about forty? Should I go higher? Okay, how about 43,000? Too many? Sadly, this is the statistic of the fatality that occurs on our roads annually. For many people, some of their family members who did not make the most recent reunion are counted in these 43,000 stolen lives.

According to a 2002 Preliminary Estimates of Highway Fatalities from the United States of America Department of Transportation (U.S. DOT), "42,800 died on the nation's highways in 2004, up slightly from 42,643 in 2003." This article also indicates that "...traffic crashes continue to be the leading cause of death in American children and young adults." Since speeding is second nature to many drivers, you should know that "Speeding continues to be cited as a major factor in almost one-third (31 percent) of traffic fatalities nationally..." according to the 2005 Survey of The States on speeding conducted by the Governors Highway Safety Association (GHSA). Interestingly, you are partly responsible for paying to take care of the clean up. How so? Think of your insurance premium and taxes you pay each year. The U.S. DOT article mentioned earlier states, "...traffic crashes come at an enormous cost to society...NHTSA estimates show that highway crashes cost society $230.6 billion a year ... " This price tag is more than two times the amount President Bush initially requested from Congress in his State of the Union speech following the end (Shock and Awe engagement) of the war in Iraq. Of the $230.6 billion, speed-related fatalities run away with about "$40 billion each year," as reported in the GHSA 2005 Survey of The States report.

What the Officials Say

Apart from the monies spent on these crashes, the number of injuries that occur on our roads annually is shocking. In response to the issue of speeding and traffic safety, several government and private agencies met in Washington, DC, on June 15–16, 2005, to review and suggest some protocols for a reduction in speed-related fatalities. They reported that speeding claimed 13,380 lives in 2003 and 13,087 in 2004.

From the National Highway Traffic Safety Administration (NHTSA) was the director of the Office of Research and Technology, Richard Compton. Mr. Compton expressed, "Speeding-related traffic fatalities have remained essentially unchanged since 1992, accounting for ... about 13,000 lives annually," ("National Forum on Speeding"). Do the math. From 1992 to 2006 is fifteen years. Thus a minimum total (15 X 13,000) is 195,000. Nearly 200,000 lives were eliminated due to speeding by the end of 2006, not including all the other causes of motor vehicle fatality. Apart from these fatalities, we can expect about three million injuries annually, and what will this be if we multiply it by fifteen? These numbers make us seem as though we are our own terrorists.

The senior vice president for research for the Insurance Institute of Highway Safety (IIHS), Dr. Susan Ferguson, in the same meeting in DC, indicated that the risk of injury and fatality increases exponentially as crash speeds increase. Talk about high school math playing a major role in real life! Yet many drivers fly past others all the time. It seems as the speed limit increases on a particular roadway, many drivers increase their speed by at least 10 mph beyond the limit. For some reason some of them believe the posted speed limit is the minimum you are allowed to go, and "woe be unto the obedient driver" who drives at the speed limit. He is considered a road hazard and a threat to public safety.

Two Primary Sources of Information

NHTSA uses two primary data systems for gathering and analyzing traffic crashes of all severity. One of these systems is the Fatality Analysis Reporting System, better known as FARS, and is most recognized and often used by government agencies and private organizations. FARS, according to the NHTSA National Center for Statistics and Analysis (NCSA) Traffic Safety Facts 2004 report, was "Established in 1975 ... contains data on the most severe traffic crashes, those in which someone was killed." Moreover, "To be included in FARS, a crash must involve a motor vehicle traveling on a traffic way customarily open to the public, and must result in the death of an occupant of a vehicle or a nonmotorist within thrity days of the crash." The other data system is the National Automotive Sampling System-General Estimates System, otherwise known as GES. Established in 1988, GES, unlike FARS, data are "probability samples ... ," according to the 2004 report. GES data involve all types of severity, and not primarily fatality crashes like FARS.

While GES data is a collection of Police Accident Reports (PAR) that involve crashes that range from property damage to the loss of human life, "FARS data are obtained solely from the state's existing documents:"

Police Accident Reports	Death Certificates
State Vehicle Registration Files	Coroner/Medical Examiner Reports
State Driver Licensing Files	Hospital Medical Reports
State Highway Department Data	Emergency Medical Service Reports
Vital Statistics	Other State Records

Traffic Fatality and Injury History: Know the Story (From 1966–2004)

On May 20, 1999, America was rocked and in tears by the massacre that occurred at Columbine High School in Littleton, Colorado. This tragedy claimed the lives of fourteen students and one teacher. For days our nation mourned the loss of our own as we pondered in disbelief of an event such as this happening in our schools. While fifteen people's lives were ended as a result of this event, nearly 43,000 people are losing their lives annually on our roads.

NHTSA NCSA Traffic Safety Facts 2004 report chronicles the trend from 1966 to 2004 of all reported fatal crashes, and the trend from 1988 to 2004 of all reported injury crashes. The following table shows the year, fatalities, injuries, vehicle miles traveled in billions, and fatality and injury rates per 100 million vehicle miles traveled. This is a modified table, so a few categories were excluded, but you may view the actual document online at the address found in the reference section (see reference #4).

Modified Table 2 From NHTSA Traffic Safety Facts 2004 Report (page 15)

Persons Killed or Injured … Vehicle Miles Traveled, 1966–2004

Year	Fatalities	Injured	VMT (billions)	Fatality Rate per 100 Million VMT	Injury Rate per 100 Million VMT
1966	50,894	-	926	5.50	-
1970	52,627	-	1,110	4.74	-
1975	44,525	-	1,132	3.25	-
1976	45,523	-	1,402	3.25	-
1977	47,878	-	1,467	3.36	-
1978	50,331	-	1,545	3.26	-
1979	51,093	-	1,529	3.34	-
1980	51,091	-	1,527	3.35	-
1981	49,301	-	1,555	3.17	-
1982	43,945	-	1,595	2.76	-
1983	42,589	-	1,653	2.58	-
1984	44,257	-	1,720	2.57	-
1985	43,825	-	1,775	2.47	-
1986	46,087	-	1,835	2.51	-
1987	46,390	-	1,921	2.41	-
1988	47,087	3,416,000	2,026	2.32	169
1989	45,582	3,284,000	2,096	2.17	157
1990	44,599	3,231,000	2,144	2.08	151
1991	41,508	3,097,000	2,172	1.91	143
1992	39,250	3,070,000	2,247	1.75	137
1993	40,150	3,149,000	2,296	1.75	137
1994	40,716	3,266,000	2,358	1.73	139
1995	41,817	3,465,000	2,423	1.73	143
1996	42,065	3,483,000	2,486	1.69	140
1997	42,013	3,348,000	2,562	1.64	131
1998	41,501	3,192,000	2,632	1.58	121
1999	41,717	3,236,000	2,691	1.55	120
2000	41,945	3,189,000	2,747	1.53	116
2001	42,196	3,033,000	2,797	1.51	108
2002	43,005	2,926,000	2,856	1.51	102
2003	42,884	2,889,000	2,890	1.48	100
2004	42,636	2,788,000	2,963	1.44	94

Wow! What was going on from 1966–1981 with the fatalities? I believe that you already know the answer. There were no mandatory seat belt laws amongst the states, as well as no major campaigns to arouse the public's attention. In fact, it took until 1984 for New York to become the first state to enact the mandatory seat belt law, which became effective in 1985, based on data obtained from the New York State Department of Motor Vehicles Governor's Traffic Safety Committee's website (see reference #5). This site indicates "…approximately 16% of individuals wore seat belts," that year (1984) and, "…1012 people who were unrestrained died in motor vehicle crashes." It also states, "In 1985, the year the seat belt law went into effect, the compliance rate was 57%, and unrestrained deaths dropped to 644."Thus, we see obedience actually saved hundreds of lives. Further statistics show that the seat belt compliance rate in New York went from 71% in 1993 to 85% in 2003, and increased to 86% in 2004.

As shown in the modified table above, the fatality rate from 1966 to 1981 was well above 2.5, meaning that for every 100 million vehicle miles traveled, we expected about three or more deaths to occur. Today many drivers who speed argue that the fatality rate has dropped significantly, thus proving speed does not kill. But what they fail to realize is we are living in a technologically advanced society where vehicles are manufactured with many more safety features, such as ABS brakes, dual front air bags, side impact air bags, and much more. With these features many drivers are nonchalant about obeying the speed limit. They feel safe, so they do as they please, some driving well above 90 mph, regardless of imminent danger, and some are members of the Century Club (speeds of 100 mph).

Look at the injured category again. We see that it decreased by about 23% from nearly 3.5 million in 1988 to approximately 2.7 million in 2004, but the fact is, it is high. We are talking about millions here! Many people are happy to get a million dollars. This is a fact because we see here in Georgia, many gravitate to playing the Georgia Lottery in hopes of winning millions.

When we warn drivers to wear seatbelts, and tell them do not drink and drive, do not speed, and to drive responsibly, many laugh cynically at our statements, believing we do not know what we are saying. Yet the statistics prove that many Americans are dying on the roads, while many more are seriously injured. Table 2 illustrates that about 94 people were injured in a traffic crash for every 100 million vehicle miles traveled in 2004, and we learned earlier that motor vehicle crash was the leading cause of death in American children and young adults. In fact, 629 persons under five years old lost their lives in 2004, compared to 612 persons five to nine years old, and these were infants, toddlers, and children who did nothing, but sat in the vehicles while someone else led them to their death. Another 1,364 persons ages 10–15 were eliminated via motor vehicle crashes, plus a whopping 5,896 individuals 16–20 years old who lost their lives as well. Had these individuals died from the acts of terrorists, the American public would demand its government marshal all of its resources to bring the terrorists to justice. How ever we look at it, these people are still dead, so what are we going to do?

I opened this chapter by asking how many members are in your extended family because knowing and understanding the importance of every member of your family will help you become more demanding in holding him accountable for driving responsibly and to obey the traffic laws. I know there are some drivers who would care less about who dies on the road, as long it is not anyone directly related to them. This way of thinking never profits because when terrorists look at Americans, they do not see some as Georgians, some as New Yorkers, some as Californians, and so forth. No. Instead, they lump us all into one category—their enemies. As a nation, we have lost more than 1.4 million of our own in motor vehicle crashes over the years based on Table 2. This number is a little more than the number of people who were annihilated in the genocide in Rwanda, Africa, in 1994, and more than seven times the number of people killed in the atomic bomb explosions in Hiroshima, and Nagasaki, Japan, during World War II. Also, more than 54 million Americans from 1988 to 2004 have been injured on our roads, of which about 32 million suffered from permanent damages such as a loss of one or more limbs, brain damage, and broken ribs. Who's next?

Effects of Motor Vehicle Crashes and Fatalities

There are many factors contributing to motor vehicle crashes: speeding, alcohol, reckless driving, road types and structures, and weather, just to name a few. The statistics, however, show speeding as one of the two leading causes of these crashes, less than one percent of which result in the lost of human life. I can hear a speeder saying, "You see, I told you that speeding doesn't kill, if it does, then why is the death toll for speeding less than one percent for all traffic crashes?" Well, let me ask you a question: How many people died in the World Trade Center terrorist attacks in September 2001? Some 2,900 lives were stolen in this tragedy, not including those injured. So what did we lose? We've lost these innocent souls, billions of dollars in real estate and equipment, and many Americans were terrified, even to this day. Many nations of the world mourned with us, and our economy suffered a loss of billions of dollars in the airline industry and other markets. Similarly, traffic crashes cost society about $230.6 billion, eliminate some 43,000 lives annually, about fourteen times the number who died in the terrorists attacks on September 2001, and many families are paralyzed to this day as a result. Ask the Schaefer family.

"I was a very controlling parent," Schaefer says. "But I never thought my child would be killed in a car." To this day, Schaefer frequently stays in her bedroom all day, mourning the loss of her only child ... On the 8th of every month, Schaefer visit's the spot on I-95 where her daughter was killed on July 8, 2003 ... "A mother's life is all about being devoted to her child," says Schaefer, who chose laughter as her cell phone ring tone because she so seldom hears it anymore. "One crazy night took everything away."

(O'Donnell)

Factors Leading to Traffic Fatalities and Injuries

With the rate at which many of our grandparents, fathers, mothers, brothers, sisters, and other relatives and friends are dying because of motor vehicle crashes, we can expect a loss of life every twelve minutes. This is no different from an airplane hijacker killing one hostage every twelve minutes because his demands were not met. And the sad thing about these fatalities is they were senseless and unnecessary. About every forty minutes an American loses his life due to a speed-related traffic fatality, and another life is stolen about every thirty-one minutes due to an alcohol-related traffic fatality. When are we going to stop these unnecessary killings? We, as a nation, travel the far seas to various countries to spread democracy and to ensure safety to all who support America's cause for justice and freedom from political tyrants, communism, and other fascist regimes, as well as those who eagerly pursue the possession of weapons of mass destruction, but we show no respect for human lives on our roads. We can say what we want, but the fact still remains, we are actually practicing warfare on our roads. I wonder how our American public would react if our government finds out and reports to the nation that terrorists have developed a means of programming vehicles to smash into each other at high speeds. We would want immediate action to nullify this threat. Nevertheless, we practice the very same thing on our roads. Table 65, extracted from the 2004

NHTSA NCSA Traffic Safety Facts report shows what happens when drivers and motorcycle operators did not comply with the traffic laws:

Related Factors for Drivers and Motorcycle Operators Involved in Fatal Crashes:

Factors	Number	Percent
Failure to keep in proper lane or running off road	13, 954	24.0
Driving too fast for conditions or in excess of posted speed limit or racing	11, 818	20.3
Under the influence of alcohol, drugs, or medication	7, 072	12.2
Failure to yield right of way	4, 611	7.9
Operating vehicle in erratic, reckless, careless, or negligent manner	3, 905	6.7
Inattentive (talking, eating, etc.)	3, 671	6.3
Swerving or avoiding due to wind, slippery surface, vehicle, object, no motorist in roadway, etc.	2, 666	4.6
Failure to obey traffic signs, signals, or officer	2, 607	4.5
Overcorrecting/oversteering	2, 466	4.2
Vision obscured (rain, snow, glare, lights, building, trees, etc.)	1, 679	2.9
Drowsy, asleep, fatigued, ill, or blackout	1, 653	2.8
Making improper turn	1, 537	2.6
Driving wrong way on one-way traffic way or on wrong side of road	936	1.6
Other factors	9, 420	16.2
None reported	20, 216	34.8
Unknown	780	1.3
Total Drivers	**58, 080**	**100.0**

Note: The sum of the numbers and percentages is greater than total drivers, as more than one factor may be present for the same driver.

Failure to Keep in Proper Lane

It is amazing how 13,954 or fewer drivers and motorcyclists lost their lives because they chose not to remain in the proper lane. I see it all the time. Some drivers are in such a hurry that they constantly drive as though they are playing dodgeball on the road, zooming in and out of lanes, rushing pass others and cutting them off only to get one car ahead of traffic. We call many things accidents, when in fact there really is no true accident. I alluded earlier that it is the law of sowing and reaping, the law of cause and effect.

Take boxing for instance. Yes, it is a fantastic sport, but at high cost. The human body was never made to be punched on, but it is quite entertaining to see two guys burst each other's brains out in the ring. We even get angry when our guy was unable to knock his opponent out. Imagine that: a man pounding on our head with the intent of knocking us unconscious. We arrest parents or guardians for physically abusing their children, yet the result is the same as with boxing—bruises were made and blood was shed. The only difference is the guys fighting in a boxing match have agreed to do so and are fully aware of all dangers. I am not putting down boxing, nor am I telling you not to watch it. That is not my purpose. I look at selected fights myself. All I am saying is the law of cause and effect is involved. If a 220-pound guy hits on your head with all of his might for a good thirty minutes, you should not be surprised if the doctor announces you will not be able to function well in your mind in your later years. One fight may not severely impact you now, but years later, after many fights, the law of cause and effect catches up to you. Similarly, many drivers do not see an immediate danger in driving recklessly, so they continue doing it. The problem hits us hard when it hits at our doorsteps, when someone in our own home is crippled in a motor vehicle crash and it was not his fault, when the doctor announces that he will not walk again, and we cannot get any financial remedy from the other driver because he has no insurance and is not capable of rendering financial compensation of his own.

Failure to Yield Right of Way

Table 65 above shows about 4,611 drivers and motorcycle riders lost their lives in 2004 due to a failure to yield right of way. But this is actually no surprise. America, sadly, when it comes to driving, is a nation full of law breakers. Stop means go these days. We call the stop sign a "rolling stop." It seems as though obedience is a crime, because one could get rear-ended for first stopping at a four-way stop before proceeding through the intersection. I know because I was compelled to slow down rather than stop because of drivers behind me. Some would even honk their horn at you.

If you look at every country that operates traffic light signals and four way stops, it is amazing that though we have our differences as countries, we all come to understand red means stop and green means go. I watch the drivers in my neighborhood on many occasions. They never stop at the stop signs, but slow down then continue on their way. This behavior is prevalent in some school zones. For instance, one afternoon after school was dismissed I decided to patrol the front of our school to ensure our students' safety. It was very displeasing to see parents, teachers, students, and visitors drive through the school compound without stopping at the stop signs. It was so prevalent that I asked some students who were standing there with me to observe what I saw. They were amazed! The only time these drivers stopped at the signs was when other cars were approaching the intersections. Their failure to yield right of way was enough to convince an uninformed person that stop means go. Perhaps you have seen the same thing happen in your area. But this is America, where on the roads there is really no right or wrong: just do as you please, as long as no one gets hurt.

Improper Turns

The general public sees no problem with committing illegal U-turns. Parents punish their children for not obeying the rules of the home, and teachers give a child either an N or U in conduct grade if he or she continues to be unruly, yet these parents and teachers go onto the roads and practice all kinds of dangerous driving. These children see their lack of integrity all the time. I know, because I used to do it. I remembered once our county had an early release for the students while teachers went to staff development training. After our training, I stopped by one of my cousin's homes. He and his best friend work with a teacher in the video department at their school and performed a recording for their school's staff development training that day. They remarked, "Teachers are worse than students when it comes to listening." I laughed because it was true. We punished students for failing to pay attention in class, yet we do the same in faculty meetings and staff development trainings.

Parents, your children are not fools, and they are not stupid. They only follow what you teach them. If you speed, make illegal U-turns, run red lights, and practice all other kinds of illegal driving with them in the car, they see you. They may not say anything, but it all goes into the "computer," and later, when you may not see them, it all comes out—ask their friends.

Driving Excitement

Alcohol and speeding combined are lethal when it comes to driving. "There were 16,694 alcohol-related fatalities in 2004—39 percent of the total traffic fatalities for the year ("Traffic Safety Facts 2004: Alcohol")." This document shows one alcohol related fatality every thirty-one minutes, and further indicates, "An estimated 248,000 people were injured in crashes where police reported that alcohol was present—an average of one person injured approximately every two minutes. Approximately 1.4 million drivers were arrested in 2003 for driving under the influence of alcohol or narcotics."

So why do some people drink and drive? Why do they speed? Why do they make illegal U-turns? Why do they practice dangerous driving? They do these things because for many reasons. *U.S.A. Today*, in several articles posted to its Web site in February 2004, answered the question about why people speed by saying, "...we think we have a right to," "...we think we have a good excuse," "...we're sure we won't crash—or get hurt," "...everyone else does, especially our leaders," and "...because no one's gonna stop us." In fact, in the article, "Why do we speed? Because we think we have a good excuse," the writer mentioned some excuses made by drivers in traffic court. Some drivers made excuses such as "I was picking up a sick child;" "I had to make a midnight curfew," and "I was going downhill." I once used this downhill line when I was driving to college to take an exam. I thought it was a surefire excuse, but that officer cared less about it. He gave me a ticket anyway.

Police Officers Have Heard All the Excuses

Believe me: the cops have heard all of the excuses as to why people speed. Back in April 2006, I did a ride-a-long with Officer M.B. Pension from DeKalb County Police Department, Georgia. After the officer calibrated his radar gun, we hit I-285 North. The car's state-of-the-art radar system was reading speeds ranging from 55 mph to 90 mph on this 55 mph interstate. We then merged onto Georgia 78-East and operated this road for some time. We continued our patrol on I-20 west where one driver was clocked at 79 mph on a 55 mph stretch. When the officer approached him and requested information, the driver, a male, responded, "You know Officer ___?" Officer Pension said, "Yes, I know Officer ___ very well. He calls and talks to me everyday." Feeling comfortable, the driver expressed, "Officer ___ is a very close friend of the family, and he said the only way a police would stop you is if you are extremely over the speed limit." Officer Pension responded, "Well if you keep listening to Officer ___, you will continue to get tickets."

As for the "Everybody speeds" excuse, never use this before an officer. There is a famous story about this one.

> A man was going well beyond the speed limit when an officer clocked him and began pursuit. The man noticed blue lights flashing in his rearview mirror and pulled over. When the officer approached the man's car and asked him for his license and registration, the man said, "But Officer, everyone else is speeding." The officer asked him, "Have you ever been fishing?" The man said, "Yes, I have!" At this the officer asked, "Ever caught all the fish?"

> In other words, police officers will catch as many offenders as possible. Some will escape, but others will pay. The best way not to pay is to obey the rules of the roads.

Did You Know?

People go into bondage and remain in it due to a lack of information, a lack of wisdom, and because of unwillingness to do what is right after they have learned what is right. If you do not know why you are being stolen from, why you cannot get along with people, why you were not promoted, and why things always go wrong with you, then it is likely you will continue to get the same results. People who are in debt remain there until they know and act upon new information that will lead them out of debt. Similarly, people are dying daily in motor vehicle crashes due to a lack of knowledge about the statistics of traffic fatalities, a lack of knowledge or experience of how to drive responsibly, and an unwillingness to observe to do right when they know better. Consequently, it is the innocent who ends up paying for the mistakes of the guilty.

For some people, knowing the magnitude of traffic crashes and fatalities are enough to convince them to be obedient drivers. Thus I believe you should know:

Crashes

- Nearly 6.2 million police-reported motor vehicle crashes occurred in the United States in 2004. Almost one-third of these crashes resulted in an injury, with less than 1% of total crashes (38,253) resulting in a death.

- Midnight to 3:00 a.m. on Saturdays and Sundays proved to be the deadliest three-hour periods throughout 2004, with 1,174 and 1,277 fatal crashes, respectively.

- More than half of fatal crashes occurred on roads with posted speed limits of 55 mph or more. 39% of fatal crashes involved alcohol. For fatal crashes occurring from midnight to 3:00 a.m., 76% involved alcohol.

People

- A total of 42,636 people lost their lives in motor vehicle crashes in 2004. Another 2.8 million people were injured.

- The majority of persons killed or injured in traffic crashes were drivers (64%), followed by passengers (29%), motorcycle riders (3%), pedestrians (3%), and pedal cyclists (1%).

- Persons sixteen to twenty years old had the highest fatality and injury rates per 100,000 population. Children five to nine years old had the lowest fatality rates, and children under five years old had the lowest injury rates.

- For every age group, the fatality rate per 100,000 population was lower for females than for males. The injury rate based on population was higher for females than for males in every age group, except for people over seventy-four years old.

Children

- In 2000, there were a total of 41,821 traffic fatalities in the United States. The 0–14 age group accounted for 6% (2,343) of those fatalities.

- In the United States, an average of six children 0–14 years old were killed and 797 were injured every day in motor vehicle crashes during 2000.

- In 2000, 20% of the children under fifteen years old who were killed in motor vehicle crashes were killed in alcohol-related crashes.

- Of the children 0–14 years old who were killed in alcohol-related crashes during 2000, almost half (223) were passengers in vehicles with drivers who had been drinking, with blood alcohol concentration (BAC) levels of 0.01 gram per deciliter (g/dl) or higher.

- Another eighty children under fifteen years old who were killed in traffic crashes in 2000 were pedestrians or pedal cyclists who were struck by drinking drivers (BAC_0.01 G/DL).

Pedestrians

- In 2000, 4,739 pedestrians were killed in traffic crashes in the United States, a decrease of from the 6,482 pedestrians killed in 1990.

- On average, a pedestrian is killed in a traffic crash every 111 minutes. (Pedestrians; 2000)

Vehicles

- Nearly 95% of the 11 million vehicles involved in motor vehicle crashes in 2004 were passenger cars or light trucks.

- The proportion of vehicles that rolled over in fatal crashes (20.5%) was four times as high as the proportion in injury crashes (5%) and sixteen times as high as the proportion in property-damage-only crashes (1.3%).

- Regardless of crash severity, the majority of vehicles in single- and two-vehicle crashes were going straight prior to the crash. The next most common vehicle maneuver differed by crash severity: negotiating a curve for fatal crashes, turning left for injury crashes, and stopped in traffic lane for property-damage-only crashes.

- Motorcycles in fatal crashes had the highest proportion of collisions with fixed objects (26.4%), and buses in fatal crashes had the lowest proportion (2.2%).

* These statistics were obtained from the FARS Web-based Encyclopedia Web site (see reference #9.)

Choices

The above statistics will place a concerned and uninformed parent in shock with his or her mouth opened, wondering whether his or her child might be next. Parents, children, and others have petitioned the government to do something about the needless deaths and injuries that occur on our roads. Their voices have been heard in many circles and much has been done to curtail the madness on the roads. Groups such as MADD (Mothers Against Drunk Driving) have been quite effective in bringing the awareness of drunk driving to the public's attention. But the truth is the government and these groups have no control over what citizens choose to do. We can punish speeders, drunk drivers, and other traffic violators all we want, but it is up to them to choose to do right. President John F. Kennedy announced on June 11, 1963, that, "…law alone cannot make man see right" (PBS). On our roads we see these famous words manifest exponentially when drivers do "rolling stops" and regard the maximum speed limit as a minimum, when no left turn signs are interpreted as "It doesn't matter; go ahead, do as you please," when drinking and driving is considered cool, especially among teenagers, when parents are speeding down the road and no one in the vehicle is wearing a seatbelt, when driving in the emergency lane is becoming normal during traffic holdup, and when drivers drive aggressively, endangering themselves and others. Yes, there is a law that forbids each of these actions, but many drivers pay absolutely not attention to them. Then someone gets hurt and family members must bare the burden and are crippled with grief.

Increased Speeds Mean More Deaths

"In 1973, Congress enacted what was called the National Maximum Speed Limit (NMSL) as a measure to conserve fuel during the energy crises," according to the GHSA 2005 Survey of The States Report. "The NMSL limited speeds on interstates and limited access roadways to 55 mph ... Following years of controversy over the NMSL, Congress repealed the national speed policy in 1995." This repeal meant states and local governments had the authority to regulate speed limits on these roads, which many states did by raising the speed limits. "States that raised their speed limit saw a 15 percent increase in fatalities on interstates and freeways," according to a 1999 Insurance Institute of Highway Safety (IIHS) estimate. Moreover, the Survey of the States Report indicated, " ... In the most recent report (2003), IIHS found when states increased the speed limit to 75 mph, a 38% increase in the number of deaths per million vehicle miles of travel occurred, compared to states that did not increase the speed limit. States that increased speed limits to 70 mph experience a 35 percent increase, resulting in approximately 1,100 more deaths."

How Many Speeding Tickets Can You Handle?

Brace yourself; you might be overwhelmed for a moment! But know that what follows is not unusual. What I am about to share is somewhat of an American way of life. The following numbers were extracted from the GHSA 2005 Survey of The States Report and the U.S. DOT NHTSA NCSS Traffic Safety Facts 2004 Report.

In 2004 there were 15 states that had the highest fatalities based on data gathered from the Traffic Safety Facts 2004 Report. These states were:

Alabama (1,154)	Illinois (1,356)	Ohio (1,286)
Arizona (1,150)	Michigan (1,159)	Pennsylvania (1,490)
California (4,120)	Missouri (1,130)	South Carolina (1,046)
Florida (3,244)	New York (1,493)	Tennessee (1288)
Georgia (1,634)	North Carolina (1,557)	Texas (3,583)

And in the previous year, these states showed a great example of public failure to observe the speed limit. In fact, if you are a citizen of any one of these states and your state decides to pay you 10% of its revenue generated from speeding offenders, you will be loaded in a day's span, and astronomically loaded in a year. Here is the proof:

In 2003, the State Patrol Depart, alone, according to GHSA, wrote the following speeding citations:

Alabama (105,368)	Illinois (173,080)	Ohio (431,036)
Arizona (data not specified)	Michigan (10,505 drivers in injury crashes; did not specify agency.)	Pennsylvania (196,222 convictions; did not specify agency)
California (993,592)	Missouri (125,816)	South Carolina(228,363)
Florida (396,252)	New York (no data available)	Tennessee (203,913; Highway Patrol)
Georgia (204,128)	North Carolina (360,000 est.)	Texas (578,977, statewide)

Let us assume that each citation had a fine of $100. Do you see how quickly you would become rich? If you are from California, and that state paid you 10% of just the state patrol speeding revenue, you would have walked away with 10% X $100 X 993252, which is about $9.9 million. Now include all fifty states. Talk about wasted money! It does not pay to speed! Now, consider about six million crashes nationwide with a minimum $100 fine for each. We are looking at $600 million to the nation, and your 10% would allot you $60 million. With this figure coming to you, I presume you would have quit your regular job by now. As a nation, we can do extraordinary things with this much money, but we seldom think as a unified people, and so we kill about 43,000 on our roads annually and injure nearly sixty-five times as many.

But proponents of speeding claim that insurance companies are profiting from higher premiums. But who goes into business with the intent of losing? Whether the insurance companies profit from higher premiums is irrelevant and immaterial to drivers obeying the speed limit. Remember our $9.9 million and $60 million scenario above? Well, guess how much insurance companies have to distribute when property damage crashes occur? You probably guessed right—it's in the billions annually. I have been driving responsibly for well over three years and still have a high premium. One reason is due to my early years of disobedience and another due to today's reckless drivers in my age bracket. But it is falling significantly, because my driving is evident that I am for peace and my insurance company knows that. When you decide to obey the speed limit and to drive responsibly, they will notice your kindness and reward your good behavior, as well!

In God We Trust

(Can He Trust In Us?)

The most controversial conversation to arise in our public schools today is the topic of mixing church and state. Mainly, people are widely separated when the name Jesus is mentioned in our schools. We say we are a nation that trusts in God. It is obvious that the God we refer to is Jehovah, God of the Christians. No one can refute this because it is true. In fact, if you have ever listened intently to conversations where a person is faced with grave difficultly, he would say, "Oh God!" or "Jesus Christ!" out of frustration, desperation, and fear. I have never heard someone say, "Oh Allah!" or "Muhammad!" or "Oh Buddha!" or "Oh Zoroaster!" or "Oh Bahaula!" out of frustration, desperation, and fear. Maybe people have, but it is not as frequently heard. What I am alluding to is we, as a nation, somehow call on the Almighty God when there is a problem bigger than ourselves or beyond our ability to avert. Once the problem subsides, we revert to our way of doing business.

You may disagree, but we both know it is true. I am not writing to convince you to believe in God. Rather, I am making you aware of the madness that occurs on our roads, showing you there is a more excellent way to commute out there, so we all may reap the benefits of obedience! When things are not so good, some of us run to God for help, but we turn around and do our own thing when we think we do not need Him. We see similar examples with our children. When some of them want something from us, they please us in everyway possible, sometimes to our amazement! We know they are up to something. Once they get it, they somehow forget to obey us. We as a nation, and many individuals, treat God the same way. I remember once I went to church and requested "traveling mercies" when I planned to drive from state to state, yet flew down the road as though I was traveling on the German Autobahn. Forget about safety, I had places to go and obedient drivers were a threat to my safety (at least that was what I thought), and as for cops, they were just an impediment to my enjoyment. Their punishment of linear condemnation (writing citation) only made me angry with the entire justice system. That was my mindset in those days. I had completely forgotten about my prayer request to God for keeping me safe when I was doing my thing, yet when I got a ticket for speeding, I sought Him for help in paying it!

God Is Not Responsible, Drivers Are

Some people blame God for their loved ones dying on the roads, while some say, "Well, God took him," or "God took her." But it was not God doing the taking; it was drivers who failed to do right by the traffic laws. The Weinstein, Chase, Messinger and Peters, P.C. in Brooklyn, New York, states on its Web site:

> Aggressive driving has become a serious problem on our roadways. What is aggressive driving? Most of us know it when we see it, but NHTSA, after discussing with law enforcement and the judiciary, defines aggressive driving as occurring when "an individual commits a combination of moving traffic offenses so as to endanger other persons or property."

So I am not the only one saying some drivers are out of control on the roads. Furthermore, NHTSA Administrator Jeffrey Runge, M.D., voiced his concerns by saying, "As a nation, we should be outraged over the loss of nearly 43,000 of our friends, neighbors and family members ... All of us—individuals as well as government—should resolve to make highway safety our highest public health priority" (Tyson). Similarly, former U.S. Transportation Secretary Norman Y. Mineta challenged us, "If we are ever going to reduce the needless deaths on the nation's highways, we're going to need the American public to bear greater responsibility for their personal safety" (Tyson).

So what do you say, should we blame God for the crashes on our roads? If yes, then consider the following. Tobacco companies are required by law to post labels on cigarette boxes saying smoking may contribute to cancer. We have conclusive medical reports indicating that smoking increases the risk of contracting lung cancer. Yet people smoke, despite the warnings. Should we blame the tobacco company for providing the tobacco? Some people would say yes. But the truth is the individual purchasing the product has the final decision. Yes, the tobacco company is an influence, but people have free will. That is like a person blaming the government for building more jails, saying, "The system is set up so that we go to jail." Just because they build jails does not mean that you have to go to jail. Similarly, people complain that the state lowered the speed limits to generate more revenue. Again, lowering the speed limit does not mean that you have to speed. Yes, it is uncomfortable because you are used to going at a higher speed; nevertheless, you choose to speed and get caught, or do not speed at all. The decision is always yours to make.

We are constantly being warned by the states with advertisement such as, "You drink, You drive, You lose!" and "Click It or Ticket," yet many drivers ignore them all together and get outright indignant with officers for giving them citations. If you obey the laws, then you need not be concerned with getting citations. In fact, the Apostle Paul puts it this way:

> Let every person be loyally subject to the governing [civil] authorities. For there is no authority except from God [by His permission, His sanction], and those that exist do so by God's appointment. Therefore he who resists and sets himself up against the authorities resists what God has appointed and arranged [in divine order.] And those who resist will bring down judgment upon themselves [receiving the penalty due them.] For civil authorities are not a terror to [people of] good conduct, but to [those of] bad behavior. Would you have no dread of him who is in authority? Then do what is right and you will receive his approval and commendation.
>
> (Romans 13:1–3)

What Paul said applies to every man. Yet one may say, "Well, I don't believe in the Bible, or in God, so what you are saying is foolish." But if you are an honest person, then you have to see the benefit in what Paul said by carefully analyzing the following—if we, as Americans, do not respect or keep our own laws, which we established for our safety, freedom, and enjoyment, then how can we expect our enemies to respect them? What Paul said might not convince you to believe in God, but it appeals to you respecting your own government.

A Look at History

Take for instance the World Trade Center tragedy of September 2001. People across this nation were asking, "Why?" "How could

God let this happen?" "Where was God when they hijacked those planes?" Well how come God lets a husband cheat on his wife? How come He lets a wife become unfaithful to her husband? How come He lets some women leave their babies in dumpsters? How come he lets people lie on their income taxes? How come He lets our school children and students open fire on their classmates in our public schools and colleges? How come He allows corporate fraud that leads to the loss of millions of dollars to innocent families? How come He lets some drivers drive at 130 mph, way beyond the speed limit? Where was God when Adolph Hitler and his regime annihilated nearly six million Jews, not including the other cultures of people? Where was God when one ethnic group in Rwanda, Africa, carried out genocide on another group, which resulted in nearly one million corpses while the rest of the world sat back and watched? Where was God when they dropped the atomic bombs on Hiroshima, and Nagasaki, Japan, during World War II, killing nearly two hundred thousand people (and these were not all soldiers)? Where was God when Japan attacked Pearl Harbor and killed nearly two thousand people? Where was God when they were lynching black people in America during and after slavery? Where was God? He has always been in the same place we have kept Him—the place we have left him while we were doing our own thing.

Now, He's telling us in the scriptures through the apostle Paul how to lead a peaceable and quiet life, and how to ensure our children's future by driving responsibly and in obedience to the traffic laws, but who is paying attention? People die on our roads because some drivers fail to observe the traffic laws. While the speed limit could be increased, we show no evidence that we could do and desire to do better. For instance, sometime around 2003/2004 the Georgia Department of Transportation (GA DOT) engaged in a three-year construction project on one of Georgia's most congested roads, in DeKalb County. Due to the magnitude of this project, it was dangerous for drivers to make left turns at certain parts of the road. Therefore, the DOT erected "No Left Turn" signs at these locations. Yet people drove right up to those signs, slowed down, and looked for patrol cars, before violating what the signs said. What happened to God; where was He when they did that? Why did He not make them obey? He did not and could not, because obedience is left up to us!

Someone's Life Depends Upon Your Obedience

About four years ago when He told me to stop speeding and I decided to drive at the speed limit, I knew it was for my safety, as well as other's because the way I was driving, I was trouble going somewhere to happen! I used to get mad when people obeyed the traffic laws, honking my horn for them to get out of the so-called "fast lane." Then I passed and looked them sternly in their eyes to let them know that I did not approve of their failure to allow me to pass. Oh, that was stupid! But thank God for a renewed mind!

Today, because of my obedience, many people's lives are spared. Some people would say, "So what do you think, you have control over these people's future?" Well, yes! What about the drunk drivers? Because they filled themselves up with booze and got behind the wheel, someone's mother's body is lying in the grave; someone's brother, father, cousin, and best friend are dead; some children will never see their parents again; someone's family has no peace and hates people; someone is mad with God; someone has lost their purpose for living; someone is dependant upon a machine to breathe; someone is crippled from the waist down. So did those drunk drivers play a part in those people's lives? You better believe they did. My obedience resulted in the salvation of another driver's life, and therefore I submit to you that someone's life depends upon your obedience.

Take a bank robbery, for example. Some individuals believe they should be loaded with money, and they are absolutely correct, but go about obtaining it the wrong way.

> Say four individuals walked into a well-known bank with the sole purpose of robbing the joint. They held two people at gunpoint and made demands for a female teller to empty all registers, as well as give them access to the vault, or they would shoot the two trembling customers. Shaking from fear, the teller punched a wrong digit in the passcode to the vault and created an emergency shutdown. The others watched as the lead robber became infuriated and expelled the teller's brain. Within seconds the teller's body fell to the ground, dead, while blood gushed out. With the little money they got from the registers the robbers headed for their escape car and fled the scene. The teller, still dead, was the mother of three children, two, five and nine years old.

Had those robbers decided to obey the law that teller would be alive. Now those children are without a mother, and some husband is forced to raise his children without their mother and the love of his life. I cannot begin to fathom the pain this family endured. While the robbers felt justified in what they did, this innocent wife, mother, and teller was robbed of a fruitful and long life. Let me ask you a question: how could God be pleased with the robbers' actions?

Similarly, some people drive very dangerously and without regards for others' safety, just as long as they get to their destination. Then when an emergency situation arises on the roads, they cannot avoid it because the laws of physics show no partiality. Increased speeds will increase stopping distance. Consequently, an officer must bear the burden of telling relatives that their loved one is dead due to a motor vehicle crash. What a heart-breaking report! Innocent lives perish on America's roads because some drivers do not follow the rules. These 43,000 annual traffic deaths should have never happened, but they have and continue, even to this day. Some drivers' disobedience led to the death of many others, including the death of some of those who disobeyed. What about you, whose life depends upon your obedience? Whose life depends upon your driving?

Case Studies

(The Unwelcome News)

Death of any kind can be melancholic, especially when it is a surprise. Unfortunately, many American families face this reality daily. In 2004, for instance, NHTSA NCSA "Traffic Safety Facts 2004" report indicates an average of about 3,188 fatal crashes every month (Table 23 on page 60) and an average of about 117 fatal crashes every day (Table 23 on page 61) on America's roads. The break down of these fatal crashes is as follows.

January	(2,935)	May	(3,426)	September	(3,233)
February	(2,591)	June	(3,320)	October	(3,417)
March	(2,869)	July	(3,490)	November	(3,102)
April	(3,015)	August	(3,584)	December	(3,271)

Sun.	Mon.	Tues.	Wed.	Thurs.	Fri.	Sat.
6,194	4,748	4,449	4,730	5,083	6,129	6,902

Notice these figures were higher during the months of April through August and from September through December, as well as during the weekends. In case you are trying to ascertain why, think about high school prom in March and April, as well as school and college closings from May through August, along with many other factors. Similarly, drivers were consuming more alcohol and driving under the influence of alcohol during Fridays, Saturdays, and Sundays, especially from Midnight to 3 a.m., and some teenagers consider it "cool" to party with alcohol on the weekends.

When the Doorbell Rings

Consequently, the fun turns into someone else's nightmare when an officer rings the doorbell with a remorse look on his face and must employ all of his strength to announce that a loved one was killed in a motor vehicle crash. Can you imagine what this feels like? I can only imagine what must have gone through the mind of Priscilla Estrada of Round Lake when I read of her story in the *Chicago Tribune*. Estrada's sixteen-year-old son, Salinas, had just received his learner's permit and was headed for his girlfriend's house with his best friend Rick Hernandez who was spending the night at Salinas.' His mother was so nervous about his inexperience that she hid the keys and permit. But the boys "…formed human figures by shoving mound of clothes under a comforter in the bed where they were supposed to sleep" (Gregory). Inexperience and riding with a friend proved dangerous in this story because Salinas, "lost control of the car as it barreled over a hill…It struck a tree. Both boys were killed." Salinas' mother could not believe the report that night when "…investigator Paul Forman came to Estrada's door and awoke her with the shocking news…" Going up to the boys' room was devastating. "Believe me, my heart just dropped," Forman recalled. "These were good kids. Good kids; bad choice."

The phrase "bad choice" mentioned in this article reminds me of what I see daily at school. Today, you cannot tell some students anything of value. They are not buying it. On the last day of school in May 2006, for instance, I warned one of my students not to leave the classroom before the bell or I would refer him to his administrator. Failing to follow my instructions, he excused himself and ended in a physical encounter with a security officer. We watched shortly after as a police officer cuffed him and put him in the back of a patrol car and headed for jail. His parents were burdened with having to get him out. "Good kid. Bad decision!"

Dangerous Drivers, Innocent Lives Lost

We all know dangerous driving when we see it. When a man is frustrated with traffic and hits the emergency lane, driving past everyone at 55 mph for nearly one mile before he pulls back into traffic, there is no question whether he is driving dangerously. These are some of the people who rack up a good bit of traffic convictions before the law finally deals with them fairly. This was the case of Vincent Camacho, according to the March 30, 2003, *Detroit News* article "Dangerous Drivers Killed Hundreds in Michigan." Vincent Camacho was without a doubt a dangerous driver, but the justice system failed to recognize it until he killed James Herman. Before this fatal crash Camacho had his license suspended for impaired driving. Within two months the court released him from suspension so that he could drive to work, but he ran a traffic signal and lost it again. Nevertheless, he continued to drive with a suspended license until being caught. "He piled up nine traffic convictions in three years." But April 1998 was the indicator to the courts that Camacho was Camacho. After a late-night bar engagement, Camacho hit the roads and ran a red light where he "smashed into 55-year-old James Herman…on his way home from a business trip…Herman's car flipped into the air. He died almost instantly, three miles from home." Herman's daughter, Charlene Taylor, said, "My family paid the ultimate price for the lenient sentences that kept him [Camacho] on the road. It was senseless. My dad was a good person and there was no reason for him to die." Camacho was later sentenced to eighteen to fifty years in state prison.

The article also mentioned another driver, David Scott Mulawa, who also racked up nine convictions in less than three years. However, it was his tenth violation that proved Mulawa was trouble, "…when he ran a red light on a muggy spring afternoon—that his pickup truck crashed into Stanley Frederick's door, tossed the car to the curb and left the 86-year-old retired tool maker slumped, dying over his steering wheel."

Intersection Crashes

Camacho and Mulawa are just two examples of red light violations (along with other violations) in the United States. "Intersection crashes account for more than 45 percent of all reported crashes, and 21 percent of fatalities. In 2003, 9,213 Americans lost their lives as a result of intersection-related crashes, a rate of more than one every hour" ("Intersections"). On October 21, 2006, *The Atlanta Journal Constitution* published the article "One Crash Every 2.8 Minutes," which showed the magnitude of intersection crashes in Georgia's Cobb County. "Overall, the Atlanta region is a crash machine with one traffic crash every 2.8 minutes. That includes interstates and highways, but the consequences don't stop with the people in the wrecked vehicles. The repercussions are felt far and wide. Crashes, stalls, and such incidents account for about half of all congestions on the roads…" From 2002–2004, on average, there were 550 people killed and 68,000 injured, as mentioned in this article. Also, these crashes resulted in $140,000 in property-only damage, and a whopping $4.7 billion estimated cost in terms of medical bills, lost productivity and congestion delay.

Mistakes Can Be Costly

We can punish guys like Camacho and Mulawa, but the wounds they have inflicted on innocent families are still painful, even after years of recovering. These guys' mistakes proved deadly. Sometimes we let it slip that the more responsibility one assumes, the greater the cost of his mistakes. The facts of this point can be seen from some of the decisions of some of our military generals. Some of their mistakes were buried in body bags and shipped back to the States.

Similarly, plane crashes that were the result of mistakes claimed hundreds of lives. I remember watching "The World's Deadliest Plane Crash" on Georgia Public Television, which resulted in the lost of 538 lives on that foggy day in March 1977. The captain of the KLM Flight 4805, Jacob Van Zanten, was a dedicated pilot loved by many, whose prestige was an inspiration of many pilots who were eager to be like him. The narrator expressed, "Despite his years of experience, he made a terrible mistake that will baffle experts for decades to come. He begins his takeoff without clearance from the tower. What he doesn't realize is that another plane, a Pan Am 747, is taxing on the same runway." This was a simple mistake, yet a costly one. Perhaps the captain suffered from fatigue, as the narrator assumed; nevertheless, the aftermath is still painful to some today, more than thirty years later—they have been carrying this burden longer than I have been alive. Guess what? This crash would have never occurred had some individuals chose not to rob a nearby bank that caused the lock down at the original airport where Flight 4805 was supposed to land.

You might say that no one is perfect, everybody makes mistakes. Would you hold this premise if a driver kills one member of your family everyday for the next four days in a motor vehicle crash, and then another one runs head-on with you, causing you to be on life support for years to come?

Mathematics is a subject where students make a gallimaufry of mistakes. You would wonder how they got the right answer with the wrong procedure. To some of these students, they do not care how the problem was solved—just give them the points because the answer is correct. Then they try to make the teacher feel bad for not awarding them the points. Some of my students, for instance, make statements such as, "But, Mr. Aaron, I got the right answer!"; "Does it really matter how I got the answer?"; "But it was just one wrong sign!" In their world, everyone makes mistakes and this is almost always tolerable when it comes to mathematics. From my vantage point, however, one mistake, if not dealt with, can have repercussions on a seismic scale: like entering the wrong grade into the grade book. Sometimes they would argue, "What is one wrong sign, Mr. Aaron?" to which I would respond, "Say you make a $5000 deposit into a bank account, but when you went to check your balance, it was negative $5000. What would you do?" I don't need to tell you their reaction.

It is one thing to make a classwork mistake. But the stakes are higher when the mistake pertains to the roads. Taking your eyes off traffic for a mere one second can be regretful later, if you survive. That is exactly what I did sometime around 1998, when I was returning home from college and took my eyes off the traffic just to see why the police officers and others were looking below the road next to the pavement. They were trying to get an animal out that fell through the cracks. By the time I turned to look at the car ahead of me I had run into a woman's rear bumper. They gave me a citation for following too closely. Did I make a mistake? I thought I did, but it was costly—only about a week or two earlier my mother had installed a new radiator in this car. We had to do it all over.

The way some people drive today, it makes you wonder how they got their license. In fact, Georgia's driving test can use some major modifications, especially for teens. We stick them behind the wheel and tell them to drive around the parking lot. If they did it well, they become a certified driver. But the real test is on the interstates where big rigs and other oversize vehicles scare the life out of you, compounded with some of the worlds craziest drivers, like those that signal left and turn right; those that drive in the turning lane all the way to the traffic light and then cut everyone off; those that force their way out of gas stations to make a left turn and block the traffic, while the light is green. Mistake or not, we really can do better.

Integrity Driving

(The Guarantee for Staying Alive)

Until now I have been sharing with you some unfortunate statistics of our roads and the warping effects they have and continue to manifest on the families of the victims and our economy. In this chapter, however, I will illustrate a delightfully wonderful and abundantly gratifying means to ensure your safety and that of our fellow Americans every time you commute on our nation's highways, service roads, and other roadways.

If you have ever bought a product of significant value, you probably noticed the manufacturer had a guarantee policy on the product, confirming his approval that the product will fulfill all that it was designed to do. Some manufacturers even go the extra distance by slapping a 180-day return policy on the purchase, should the product fail to meet all objectives. These manufacturers allot such long return times because they know their product will do what they say it will do. This is called confidence!

In like manner, we can have confidence in our driving, a way to drive and avoid causing crashes, speeding tickets, and many other traffic violations. This manner of driving I call "Integrity Driving." Before I go into the details of Integrity Driving, let us look at a scenario.

Say you are running late for a meeting at which your presence is vital. You have two choices: one is to obey the traffic law by keeping at the speed limit, and two is you can speed like everyone else. If you keep at the speed limit, you will be late, probably missing the entire meeting. If you speed, you can make it there just in time for the commencement. So like everyone else, you decide to floor the accelerator. What you do not see is the little girl darting out into the road to escape a dog chasing her. Before you can slam on your brakes, you had already run over her. By the time you got out of the car to aid her, she has already died. You look around and see two witnesses.

Although this is a scenario, it is very similar to many events that have transpired on our roads. You, like many other drivers, had a decision to make and apparently made the wrong one. Yes, missing the meeting was going to cost you something, but the decision to break the law now costs you more: you are charged with vehicular manslaughter. Look at the enormity of your decision:

1. the little girl is dead, a life cut short

2. her family is now in turmoil and will experience pain and grief

3. the death will cause the family members to take a few days off work and thus their employers (if they work for someone else) will lose productivity

4. you have to pay a lawyer, spend lots of time in court, and may end up behind bars

5. this crash will take a toll on your family, as well.

And the list goes on...

Some people may argue that if the owners placed a leash on the dog, then the girl would have had no need to run, and you would not have hit her. But "if" is always one step from reality. The crash did occur, and the child is dead. Yet someone might say, "It could have happened to anyone!" Unfortunately, it has happened to you, and the consequences are dire. So if you think your decisions affect only you, then reconsider; though your decisions affect you directly, they also affect others, indirectly, in the least.

What Is Integrity Driving?

The phrase "Integrity Driving" is simply the amalgamation of obedience and driving. It is doing whatever the law requires when you are on the road, provided it [the law] is applicable. What I mean by applicable is: you might be approaching a school zone on a Sunday where a flashing amber light is active and indicates you must slow to the posted speed of 25 mph, while the road speed is 35 mph. But school is out on Sunday, and no one is on campus. Somebody at the traffic safety division has forgotten to turn the lights off. You are not expected to obey this signal on non-school days.

We are living in a time when doing the right thing is considered foolish in the eyes of the majority. To accomplish their goals some resort to lying, stealing, cursing, and selling themselves short. Some students, for instance, have spent time, effort, and resources, to come up with a means to cheat on a test for which they knew they should have prepared. A man would spend time meditating on how he would rob a bank, then goes out to execute his plans, sometimes killing a few people in the process. Similarly, some drivers know that breaking the speed limit, driving dangerously, drinking and driving, tailgating, and making an illegal U-turn are unlawful, but to make up for convenience, they ignore these laws. Hence, the need for integrity in driving must be practiced.

If the speed limit is 65 mph, then drive at 65 mph or one or two miles per hour slower. But you might say, "The flow of traffic is 80 mph, so should I not keep up with the traffic?" Well, that is like a man who chooses to follow the crowd on his job, and lie on his time sheet, giving himself a few extra hours of labor. You might get away with it for now, but they will know eventually. Do you like when people mistreat you and even steal from you? Would you appreciate it if your boss knowingly gives you a check that cannot be cleared with the bank due to insufficient funds? How about if you are enrolled in a particular course and the instructor makes a mistake by giving you a failing grade when you should have received a passing grade—would you accept that? Consider the harm you might be doing to someone on the road when you choose to disregard the traffic laws. Yes, you may get away with bad driving for now, but know that the wheels of justice, they may turn ever so slowly, but when they grind, they do so ever so firmly!

Disobedience always results in selling yourself short, and someone else may end up paying for it. When we were children, some of us could not fathom why our parents wanted us to make our beds. We fussed, murmured, and got really upset, and some even made it look worse than before. Then the ice cream man came around and our parents said, "No ice cream for you. You did not make up your bed, like I told you." Had we done what they told us, we would have basked in some delicious dessert—we sold ourselves short. In like manner, when you drink and drive, someone might be killed and you will be spending years behind bars—selling yourself short. But driving with integrity will prevent the lost of life and keep you free. Think of our scenario in the beginning of this chapter. Had you driven with integrity the little girl would be alive, and you would have saved time and money, and even kept your peace of mind.

Why Integrity Driving?

Driving with integrity is necessary because it guarantees our safety, our enjoyment, our financial prosperity, and our peace of mind. Almost all motor vehicle crashes in the United States occurred as a result of driver error. Someone either was not paying attention while driving; or failed to stop at the traffic light; or to yield at the yield sign; or refused to obey the speed limit; or ignore good advice concerning drinking and driving; or did not stay in the proper lane.

Consequently, the number of crashes per year is in the millions. FARS data show that nearly 6.2 million police-reported motor vehicle crashes occurred in the United States in 2004, and an average of 6.3 million occurred in 2003, 1999, and 1998. In 1997 police officers reported more than 6.7 million crashes, down from 6.8 million the prior year. The count for 1995 and 1994 were almost 6.6 million and 6.5 million, respectively (see reference #18 for online address.) If we average two vehicles per crash with one person in each vehicle, we see a minimum average of 12,925,000 families that were impacted each of these years, ranging from property-only damage crashes to fatal crashes. So do we need integrity driving? For the sake of the numbers, we most certainly do. More so, it will grant peace of mind to millions of families. From a financial angle, do you now see how easily it is to incur a loss of $230.6 billion to our economy?

So How Do I Drive With Integrity?

I am so glad you asked this question! It shows that you are ready to make a positive change. And to help you on your quest, we will look at the three ingredients of integrity (integrity driving), as well as some of the benefits of integrity driving.

Driving "…with integrity is a threefold process" (Price). First, it means that you know what is right from what is wrong. This then will help you make a commitment to act on what you know to be right, irrespective of the cost. Thirdly, you must tell someone who can hold you accountable to what you have committed to do.

Knowing Right From Wrong

The fact that there is a right means that there is a corresponding wrong. There is a right way to make money and there is a wrong way to make money. There is a right way to talk to people and there is a wrong way to talk to people. The point is, there is a right and there is a wrong way to doing something. We all must make that distinction.

If you are going to be a person who drives with integrity, you have to know (learn) what is right and what is wrong about driving. You just cannot go with the crowd because the crowd is usually wrong. The crowd, for instance, will tell you to go with the flow of traffic. You did this and got a ticket because the cop had to pin someone. Well if the crowd was right, then no one would have gotten a ticket. Similarly, the crowd will tell you that cops do not pay attention to anyone going five to ten miles per hour over the speed limit. So you heed the crowd and end up paying because of ignorance. Again, the crowd will tell you that everyone speeds. You believe this and end up in court. The crowd was telling you everything that actually caused you to get entangled with the law. The crowd is usually wrong. In fact, the teenage crowd will tell you that seatbelts are not cool, yet they are being tossed out of their vehicles in unbelievable numbers. Thus you will actually stand to profit from knowing (learning) right from wrong when it comes to driving.

Making the Right Commitment

No soldier goes to war without his weapon! If he does, then he invites defeat. If you desire to be a soldier of integrity driving, you must make the commitment to obey the traffic laws. This means that you have to weigh the cost of your decisions to determine whether you want to pay this cost. Driving with integrity will cost you something! Nothing is free—someone has to pay. You may get something for free, but in actuality, a price was paid for you to obtain it. Are you willing to pay the price for integrity driving?

Without commitment, nothing will work to its maximum efficiency. Say a guy asks a girl to marry him and she says yes. But year after year he keeps saying, "Baby, next year we will tie the knot!" It would not be long before she says yes to another guy who asks her. The first guy's failure to make a commitment was his commitment to failure. Many people have died and many more have been severely wounded on our roads, some of whom have said, "I will slow down the next time." Unfortunately, next time never arrived. To drive with integrity you have to act instantly on what you know or believe to be right the moment you perceive it. Your mindset has to be similar to burning all bridges once you've crossed them. You burn the bridges so you do not second guess your position, so you do not come off your commitment.

Making Others Aware of Your Commitment

We are living in a time when accountability is paramount. From the classroom to the White House, our nation is demanding its citizens take responsibility for their actions. In like manner, to be a person who drives with integrity you will have to tell someone who can hold you accountable of your commitment to obeying the traffic laws. This person must be someone you can trust and who will not let you slide. You most certainly do not want to tell a friend who is strongly opposed to what you have committed to do. In all respect, that would be grossly stupid (not that you are stupid.) It would be like the woman soliciting advice about her marriage from another woman whom she knows is trying to get her husband. You know what kind of advice would be given! Look for someone of good reputation who will not suppress the truth so that your feelings would not be hurt.

Telling someone of your commitment gives you the advantage in fulfilling it because someone else expects you to do as you say, and if you truly desire to drive with integrity then you will certainly not lie about your driving. Therefore, you will have to keep your commitment. Because I constantly tell people to drive at or below the speed limit and to wear a seatbelt, I am always being observed. When they see me, they say, "Speed limit?" And since I am determined to fulfill my commitment, I tell the truth about my driving. You may argue, "No one tells the truth anymore; everybody lies." Well, that is not my confession, it is yours.

In addition, once this person knows of your commitment, he knows where you stand. Your voice on a matter lets others know whether you are for it or against it. Similarly, your silence on a matter lets them know whether you are for it or against it. For example, say you are in a car with a few friends and before the driver pulls off someone outside says to him, "Put on your seatbelt." The driver, however, drives off without buckling up and says, "Seatbelts aren't cool! Who wears seatbelts?" Now you are in the back of the car, and though you believe it is right to wear a seatbelt, you did not object to the driver's response. What impression do you believe the driver received from your silence? You got it—though you did not agree with his decision, he thought you agreed by virtue of your silence. Telling someone of your commitment will let him know exactly where you stand.

Setting Good Standards for Yourself

Driving with integrity means you will have to establish rules that you will keep. It is better for you to rule over your inner man (your spirit) than be entangled with the law because of a lack of self-control. You will have to tell yourself that if your closest friends or supporters desert you because of your commitment to doing what is right, you will finish the course alone. I told you earlier that integrity driving will cost you something. For one thing it will cause you to look stupid in the eyes of some, if not many. I know because I have had some of my family members to laugh at me. Some even argued that *I* was the hazard. Also, some drivers honk their horns at me repeatedly. Then when they got tired of tagging along, they broke the law by passing. One guy overtook me and lifted his middle finger. He probably thought that hurt me, but I already counted the cost for my commitment to doing what was right. If I had not counted the cost, it would have caused me to reconsider my position, and probably revert to a stance that I now have total control over. You know what it is—road rage! Sometimes I laugh at the rage some drivers work up while being stuck in traffic. People say "Patience is a virtue." But I have seen road rage eat away at many drivers' patience.

I cannot tell you the last day that I had road rage. The reason for my peace of mind and self-control is due to the fact that I have chosen to set and keep rules concerning my driving. When drivers cut me off, I bless them because they do not know any better. It is amazing how quickly some drivers lose it out there. In December 2006, for instance, one driver shot an eighty-seven-year-old woman on a Georgia highway because she was driving too slow for him. Similarly, some drivers have even gotten out of their cars in traffic to make statements at others who got in their way. Woe be unto the driver who keeps stopping because he is trying to look for a particular building. I remember attending a mathematics teacher staff development in August 2006. During our lunch break I decided to ride with another teacher from another high school. As we were returning from lunch, a driver kept stopping as though he wanted to turn left into a parking lot. Oh, what a mistake this driver made. My colleague began honking her horn, running her mouth as though she wanted to exit the car to get to the other driver's car. I sat cool in the front passenger seat and pointed out that she should remain calm. She responded, "Oh, I am calm!" But she kept going on and on. Now I had to deal with the nagging while the other driver went his way. I really thought this teacher was going to lose it because she would not let it go with remarks such as " ... they should get a map if they don't know where they are going!" I got to thinking, *If this is not road rage, what is?*

Never Compromise Your [Good] Standards

Life gets easier when your good standards are upheld. King Solomon once said,

"The integrity of the upright will guide them ... " (Proverbs 10:9)

This is such a true statement. In my driving, my integrity keeps me from reeling in a bunch of speeding tickets, from running red lights, running stop signs, drinking and driving, making illegal U-turns, and much more. Because I practice integrity driving daily, I do not have to think about doing what is right when I am behind the wheel. It is like second nature. I am to the point now in my driving where I do obey the traffic laws for many reasons beyond the fact that they are the law. I obey them because they are right and ensure safety both to others and myself. If an officer pulls me over, it must be for something I am really not aware of, and that has happened. But he cannot pull me over for speeding, reckless and/or aggressive driving, running stop signs and red lights, or drinking and driving because I do not compromise my standards and my will to obey the laws to the extent of my knowledge. I said earlier that integrity requires knowing right from wrong. Today you cannot go to court claiming ignorance. Seldom will a driver get off with this defense. So the best thing to do is to set standards you will keep, because they will prevent you from having to say "I am sorry" in the end.

If you do not set good standards to guide your actions, then you make yourself vulnerable to all kinds of trouble, and we see examples of these on the roads daily. Some drivers say, "I know speeding is wrong, but I cannot be late." Think about it like this: if you get pulled over by an officer for speeding, you will be late. If you crash and die, then you will always be late. On the other hand, if you have your good standards intact you may even learn how to prioritize your time and leave a little early. If you do not believe good standards for driving will be to your advantage, consider the following.

> Say a guy tells his wife that he is going to the supermarket to get a few items. While in the store, he notices a beautiful woman in the same aisle smiling at him. What she doesn't notice is his wedding ring that is covered by the handle of his shopping basket. So he returns the smile. She is blushing and turns to put an item back on the shelf. The moment she turns, this guy yanks his ring off his finger and shoves it into his pants pocket. As they move closer, he nods at her. She says hello. With strong courage he walks over to her and compliments her hair. She is taken! The smile leads to an interesting conversation, which leads to an exchange of numbers. As the days went by, phone conversations led to a walk in the park, which led to more phone conversations in the mornings, at noon, in the evenings, and during many late nights. Before you know it he is at her house. Three months later she invited him to a well-prepared dinner guaranteed to satisfy the most discriminating palate! It was at this moment that she gave him the news: "I am pregnant." Instantly, his countenance fell! The spoon went

back into the plate and remained there. He asked if the child was his. They argued back and forth on the probability of him being the father. She was confident it was his, because she knew no one else.

You get the picture, right? It all started with his compromise of his good standards. Because he was unwilling to keep his standards concerning his marriage, he and his wife, and their children, if they have any, must now pay a high price for his few moments of pleasure. Had this guy kept his ring on his finger *and* not explored the possibility of the woman's intentions, he would have never experienced the consequences. In like manner, you too, if you set good standards relative to your driving and keep them, will never have to deal with an officer for an offense you are fully aware of. It is better to restrict yourself from the instant pleasures of high-speed driving and other traffic violations than to be held behind bars and have your license suspended.

Waiting for the right circumstances to commit to obeying the traffic laws is dangerous. Those circumstances will never be right. This is similar to the kid who keeps putting off studying for a class until he gets enough time to do so. He is living in a fool's paradise. I see it every day. Some students wait until the day before a major exam to study. When the test is returned, they get angry with the teacher. They argue about why the teacher took off so many points on a particular problem. What they do not realize is they invested very little into doing well in the class. It is like the man who waited two years before his retirement to start preparing for it. He desires $10 million from his retirement package but invested $10,000 within the last two years of working. Then he gets upset with the investment company because the account does not have that much money in it. Hence, telling yourself that you will stop speeding the next time, or that this is your last drink, or you will do the right thing if you are not late, weakens your will to doing it. The fact that you choose not to do the right thing now is evident that you favor doing the wrong thing, irrespective of the cost. By doing this you are strengthening your will towards doing the things that will cost you dearly. On the other hand, by choosing to drive with integrity you will be able to escape the negative vicissitudes of life in traffic.

When terrorists attacked us on our shores, we retaliated. We deployed thousands of men on their territory, looted them with a gallimaufry of bombs and fire power, and vigorously pursued them for months. Our retaliatory efforts proved that we did not appreciate what they did. Now we are fighting the war on terror. It is abundantly clear that our standards show we do not tolerate terrorism. What will happen if we begin to act in ignorance of terrorist plots and schemes? Some terrorists are now committed to blowing up the White House. So if we compromise our standards against their unrelenting and deadly acts towards us, the result will certainly not be favorable [for us.] In the same way, you cannot allow your will towards obeying the traffic laws to be compromised. As jail is to a prisoner, so is your good driving standards to you. They both restrict you. That is why you have to set good standards for your driving, so that they will restrict you from ever getting into trouble, and keep you out of jail or the grave.

Integrity Driving Says Many Things about You

Some people say, "A picture speaks a thousand words." How? It's just a picture. You can actually tell a lot about the time and culture captured by a picture. Although pictures do not talk (as in the truest sense of the word "talk"), they do reveal a message. Similarly, your obedience in observing and keeping the traffic laws says a lot about you.

For one thing, your integrity in driving says that you value life so much that you are willing to commit yourself to ensuring others'

safety. We know that drinking does affect a driver's ability to properly operate a motor vehicle. These people run into telephone poles,
trees, and other vehicles. Many times the result is fatal. Not only do
they cut short their very lives, but also that of another. When you
choose, however, to say no to drinking and driving, you are actually
saying, "I love and value my fellow Americans so much that I am
willing to do what is right so that they may not have to experience
pain and grief as a result of my driving." When I started integrity
driving, I was not thinking mainly of others' safety. I really did not
want to pay more money to the justice department. But continuing
in it, I develop a greater love for people and want to see them safe
and enjoy life.

Secondly, your integrity in driving says that you honor our men and
women in law enforcement. One of the core values of our military
is *honor*. Until I chose to develop integrity in my driving, I had no
clue what honor meant. I heard military officers and others use it
continually, but I had no sound understanding of its magnitude and
application. I am to the point now where I want all of our officers to
be well taken care of. No more do I want to hear another officer got
shot because some unruly person refused to be ticketed for running
red lights and driving aggressively. These men and women daily
risk their lives to see to it that no harm befalls you or your family.
Some of them have even been hit by other drivers while issuing
tickets to violators. We get reports all the time about some of our
soldiers being killed in battle, losing their limbs, or being blown
into pieces by rocket- propelled grenades. Such news is unwelcom-
ing and heart-breaking. Thousands of families are in turmoil right
now as a result. These service men and women have put their lives
in the line of fire to ensure our continued freedom, prosperity, and
safety. In the same way, our law enforcement officers are risking
their very lives for us. So when you obey the traffic laws, you are

saying to them, "I truly value your service towards me. Thank you for your commitment!"

Furthermore, when you drive with integrity, you are saying to your family that you love them. How would you take it if a friend says to you, "I love you!" but then turns around and breaks into your home, steals your jewelry, some clothes, and physically injured those who reside with you? You will begin to question this friend's love. If this friend really loves you, why would he hurt you? Or take the husband who tells his wife that she is the best thing that has ever happened to him and that he loves her abundantly. Then this guy turns around and physically abuses his wife. Where is the love that he was preaching? Do you see how this principle applies to driving without integrity? When you tell your family "I love you," then drive as though you are trouble going somewhere to happen, you are actually telling them that you do not care about what they have to deal with if you should perish behind the wheel. You may say that you will never crash, but it is also the responsibility of other drivers to do what is right. What about the 1.4 million whom have perished behind the wheel since 1988, were all of them obeying the traffic laws? Not at all, someone disobeyed. Someone said by his/her actions, "I will not operate in love," and lives were stolen. Know that love never fails, never harms others, and it sees the best in all people. So when you drive with integrity by obeying the traffic laws continually, you are saying to your family, "I love you and I show it by driving in obedience to the law."

Fourthly, integrity driving says that you are trustworthy and respectful. Do you test the milk in the grocery store for poison or take it to a chemist to check for other harmful chemicals? No, not at all! You take those producers at their word. Whatever the label says, you run with it. You do not even open it and pour some out to determine whether it is good. The label is good enough. See driving the same way. Many drivers assume other drivers have a valid driver's license and are fully insured. They trust that these drivers will do the right thing. For example, when the light turns green, you proceed through, believing other drivers will not run the red light. Unfortunately, this respect is not accepted by some drivers. Because they are running late, they choose to ignore what is right in order to make up for convenience, and if that means run the light, make an illegal U-turn if no cop is visible, tailgate others and drive aggressively, or drive in the emergency lane and in the turning lane, then so be it. And one of the sad things about all of this is the children are riding with them, and witness their complete disregard for what is right.

The Best Teacher

Have you ever done the wrong thing only to realize a small still voice inside of you, which you ignored, was trying to point you in the right direction? Then you got into a fix and ended up paying much more than what you would have if you had only listened to that small still voice? There have been times when I was teaching my students a concept and I got the urge to redirect my delivery methods. I have not always listened; then I thought to myself, *Why did I not listen?* At this time it was too late; the entire class was confused, and sometimes I ended up confused with them because they would ask questions that I did not anticipate. Let me tell you, these were not pleasant times because their morale was out the window. I had to spend the rest of the period, if not another day, to get them back on track.

Many times we are faced with decisions about driving and our conscience tells us to do the right thing, but we do not always listen. You might be driving along a straight stretch of road, for example, and for some reason the urge to slow down arises, since the speed limit is way below what you are traveling. Nevertheless, you ignore the warning. Next thing you notice are flashing blue lights pulling out from behind a bridge that obscures your vision. It is too late now; you should have listened to that soft voice a moment ago.

Some people say that experience is the best teacher, and that if you had not experienced what you have, you would not know what you know now. Well, I disagree with that assessment. Experience is a teacher, but not the best teacher. I believe, rather, that obedience is the best teacher. Driving with integrity gives a more pleasant experience than failing to acknowledge what is right. I do not need to fill myself up with alcohol then get behind the wheel to figure out that drinking and driving is a dangerous combination. No. I saw a driver on the news that did this and ran head-on with another vehicle, killing both himself and the other driver. One of the virtues of being smart is learning from other people's mistakes. I submit, therefore, that doing what is right is the best teacher. By doing what is right on the road you will have a more fulfilling experience.

If experience is the best teacher, then we should thank the terrorists for 9/11 because it really helped us to become stronger and to learn how to appreciate each other; it helped so many of us to go back to church and to turn back to God; it helped so many of us to believe in the cause of American democracy; it helped us to stand up as one. Again, if experience is the best teacher, then we should not feel bad that our children are not learning as they ought. Also, if your family is very strong and united, then having it disintegrate into a dysfunctional family would be a good experience for you because you would be able to see how precious each member really is. Do you see why experience is not always the best teacher? I concur that experience will teach you some valuable lessons, but you do not need to get into a fix to learn what you could have ascertained by doing what is right. Getting a speeding ticket will teach you that it costs to disobey the law, but you could have learned that without getting a ticket. Just don't speed, and take that money you would have paid towards a speeding ticket or any other violation and invest it. Over time, you will see the increase. Hence, I submit once again that living by experience is not the best teacher, but driving with integrity illustrates a greater purpose and guarantees a richer life on our roads.

You Are Important
(Born To Make A Positive Difference)

When I think of all of those family members and friends who have lost their lives in motor vehicle crashes, my heart mourns with their families because these families will never see their love ones and friends again. If only I could change what happened. But the truth is I cannot, but I can change what happens from now.

Why Were You Born?

If you have read this book all the way to this point, then you should come to believe that my purpose is to inform you about the reality of our roads, and to inspire and encourage you to become more responsible in observing and honoring the traffic laws. The fact is Americans are dying and being injured in cinematic proportions when it comes to driving. However, the truth is we do not have to die nor be injured on our roads, because each driver does possess the ability to practice integrity, and was born to make a positive difference and to accomplish great things! Do you believe this? Do you truly believe that you were born to succeed in this life and to accomplish great things? The truth is we are all important. We were all born to live a marvelous life and to make a positive difference in this world. We all have a wonderful purpose for living!

I am so glad that I made the decision several years ago to develop integrity where my driving is concerned, and because of this, someone, including myself, is reaping the benefits. When a baby is born, the parents, family members, and their friends gather around in triumphant celebration, knowing that this child brings joy to the family and is born to be great and accomplish wonderful things! These family members and friends bring lots of gifts to honor the parents and the newborn. This proves that we do believe that we are important and that we are destined for greatness.

Now consider the following. Years later someone snuffs out this child's life in a motor vehicle crash. The fact that the person died in the crash is bad enough, but to die and not fulfill your purpose in life is worse. Take a high school graduate, for example. It is graduation day, and many family members have arrived in town to attend the graduation and to celebrate a milestone. At the dinner celebration, some members asked the grad what he intends to do in life, to which the response was, "I will be attending college in the fall to become a medical doctor. I also plan to have my own businesses and make lots of money, and I plan to get married in four years." Everyone at the table is moved with joy and cheers this ambitious family member. The weeks following the graduation, the parents received devastating news as two police officers rang their doorbell and share with them that their child [the college-bound student] was in a car crash and died on the spot. The officers watched in tears and remorse as the mother became weak and fainted while the father broke down. The other siblings, old enough to understand what has happened, cry with disbelief as they seek comfort in their father's arms.

Now let me ask you two questions. Was this graduate an important person, and did his life mean anything? Did the world benefit from all that he was to become? You are right, this graduate was important because others were severely impacted by his death. Even the officers were in tears, and it is sad that his ambition of becoming a medical doctor was never fulfilled.

Born To Make a Positive Difference

Think of all the pioneer medical doctors who have discovered and contributed a wealth of knowledge in medicine. Think of those who have spent years performing and perfecting procedures for laser eye surgery, triple-bypass heart surgery, and the many other medical procedures known to us today. Think of the intellectuals who have spent time and resources developing and producing advanced medical technology to aid in the emergency rooms. What would this world look like had these people never existed? How long would it be before we have gained the knowledge and understanding we now possess?

Think about the advances in banking and the stock market trading services; think about the means we have developed in air transportation, space adventure, and cellular phone communications; think about the discoveries made in just the computer industry in the last ten years and how we are able to compose and transmit emails in a matter of seconds, as well as to track the stock market and weather changes at any moment, and to view our bank accounts 24/7/365. We can continue this list for a very long time. The point is, these discoveries and inventions came about because of the wonderful people whom have spent time in the pursuit of their calling in life. Had they been eliminated in motor vehicle crashes before their discoveries and inventions, where would we be? That is why you must believe that your life is valuable. This world is yet to experience a marvelous discovery because you are alive. Hence, you stand to profit when you agree to drive with integrity. There is absolutely no profit in aggressive and other kinds of dangerous driving. Your life is far too important, whether you know or believe it. If others choose to believe in your potential, how much more powerful and rewarding will it be when you believe in what you are capable of contributing. The aftermath of tragedies and other defining moments in history prove that we are a people destined for greatness, and these moments also show us who was among us before their lives were stolen.

Some people say that the grave yard is the richest place because of all the talents that are buried there, talents that were robbed of the opportunity to be fully developed. We ponder and ask God why bad things keep happening to people and to our nation; why many young men die even in their teens; why children disrespect their parents, teachers, and elders; why the jails are flooded with people like never before; why people continue to rob banks, lie to each other, and show no respect for other lives. The answer is simple: many have not yet come to the realization of who they really are, what they are capable of becoming, and many do not value their own lives, so they see no value in the lives of others.

Think about it, had Adolph Hitler chose to walk in love and to obey international treaties, millions of lives would have been saved. Similarly, had Americans chose to respect each other and to honor our police officers and construction workers, as well as to observe the traffic laws, more than 54,000,000 lives would have never been severely injured as a result of motor vehicle crashes. In Washington, DC, thousands of tourists and visitors pay homage annually to the men who died in the Vietnam War during the 60s. They place flowers and pictures along the memorial wall that bears the names of some 58,000 soldiers died or pronounced missing-in-action (MIA) in that war. Someone might reason, "Had we not gone to war, these men would be alive." In like manner, if people did not drink and drive, if they did not speed and drive recklessly, if they did not disregard the red light, if they did not speed around sharp curved roads, perhaps 43,000 lives per year since 1975 might be here with us. Our fathers, mothers, brothers, sisters, and others, perhaps they would still be laughing with us. Had someone respected the laws of the roads, these people might be driving today and probably fulfilling their purpose in life. Our obedience will guarantee someone's enjoyment of life and allow them to fulfill their destiny! Wouldn't you want to fulfill yours?

Making Midcourse Corrections

During an airplane flight, the pilots must be knowledgeable and skillful in understanding the instruments in the cockpit and be able to make what is called "midcourse corrections." Due to turbulences in the air, the plane may be blown off course. Being off course by as little as one degree could put the plane many miles from its destination. Therefore, these pilots must make periodic adjustments in their course heading to ensure they reach their destinations in very little time as possible.

If you honestly admit to yourself that you do practice speeding or drinking and driving, or reckless or aggressive driving; or if you practice running red lights; or if you fail to stop at the stop signs; if you do practice driving without restraint (seatbelt) and/or insurance; or if you fail to encourage those who ride with you to wear their seatbelts, then you are running the risk of being blown off course in life that may put you and others in a destination you may not like. Like the pilots, you can make corrections to your life's heading right this moment. All it takes is your willingness and obedience to do what is right. As mentioned in the chapter titled "Integrity Driving," to drive with integrity, you must first recognize what is right from what is wrong about driving; then you must weigh the cost of doing what is right and make a commitment to doing what is right. Finally you must share your commitment with others who are worthy of holding you accountable to sticking to that which you have committed. Yes, it will cost you something, but the reward is delightfully wonderful!

If you know there is a need to make some adjustments in your driving, then you must make the commitment to drive with integrity. Make a midcourse correction, and the best time to do so is the moment you realize you are off course—right now. Do not put it off for the next time you are behind the wheel because all of the conditions may not be perfect (like being early to work,) and you will run the risk of falling victim to the circumstances. Make the decision now, write it down and place it in your room, in your vehicle, and in every place that will allow you to remember what you have committed to do. By doing this, you will be on your way to your expected destination—fulfilling your purpose in life—and many will also benefit from your obedience and the corrections you have made. I am a witness of this wonderful life, and it will be even more glorious when you are well acquainted with this peace-driven lifestyle of integrity driving.

There are many influences, but "Only you can effect change in your life!"

For Parents

(About Teen Driving)

Lately, our news media has become increasingly concerned about teen motor vehicle crashes and fatalities. It seems that on every television news station you turn to and in every newspaper you read, someone is talking about the increased teen fatalities. Many parents with teen drivers are on high alert and searching for an answer that will curb teen motor vehicle crashes. New laws are rippling across the country at every level of government in hopes of curtailing the number of motor vehicle crashes and fatalities involving teen-drivers and their passengers. Lately, a series of new initiatives have been instituted to help prevent the tragedies that stem from teen-driving and some parents are buying into these programs. I write this chapter because I believe that both parents and their teen drivers will benefit from the information I am about to disclose.

My Students' Perspectives

I interact with high school students five days a week for thirty-six weeks each year. They talk about everything, from life at home to fun at the party and dance clubs—yes, they go to the clubs with fake IDs. Since I was working on this book, I determined it was necessary to get some of their perspectives about driving and the rules under which they must operate a vehicle. Let me tell you, the responses were as varied as the number of states in this country. Some believed that parents placed too many restrictions on their driving, while some felt the government was too lenient in some states. Some believed that stricter laws will help while some believed there were too many invasions of their privacy concerning driving. We read news articles, watched some videos and the movie *License To Kill*, and listened to some who shared their family motor vehicle tragedy then they wrote critical analysis papers on their findings, as well explained why their driving matters.

In the end, after seeing the videos and the movie, and listening to some of the discomfort experienced by some of their peers, they determined that driving was much more than what they originally thought. Some did not want to drive until they turn seventeen, while some could not wait to get their license. In one class I inquired, "If you feel that your driving does matter, and that you ought to obey the rules, why do you ignore them when you drive; why so many teen deaths?" At this point they turn on each other. I laughed because all it took was a question that aroused their conscience. They began to share how some students just do not care and they should not be at the wheel. One girl even shared that one of her friends lied on the test concerning her poor vision. I listened intently because I got the opportunity to look into their minds to see how they perceive laws, as well as what they valued. It was amazing! Nevertheless, talk is cheap if you are not willing to back it with your actions. To say that you will obey the traffic laws without making a commitment to them, as we have learned in chapter four, is futile, because the circumstances will certainly derail you from your goal.

Parents Driving By Example—Required!

I submit that teen driving can be pleasant to parents if parents set the example. That means parents must first become the example. Children in this day and age do not listen to "Do what I say and not what I do!" Please do not use this line when illustrating to your teen driver about the importance of driving responsibly. As a teacher, I witnessed firsthand that my students are as studious and responsible as I am. If I demonstrate by example how to keep a proper notebook, you know, the one where you can find everything in the proper sequence, theirs will look the same. Before I illustrated what a good notebook looked like, I was getting packets of work. Some of my students could not tell the difference between a notebook and a textbook because they have always placed their notes inside of the textbook so that everything was together, until I threaten to revoke the text and have them submit the homework exercises. So parents, you have to be the example of what you desire your teen driver to become.

But the way some parents drive, it leaves one to speculate. In some of my interviews drivers recalled watching the news and saw a woman breast feeding her baby while driving. I have seen some parents pick up their children from school and neither the parents nor the children were buckled up. We send our children to school or home school them because we believe that if we share knowledge with them, they will learn something they did not know, something that will benefit them in years to come. The same principle applies to driving. Your driving is knowledge for your teen. So if you drink and drive, since some children do not do as parents say but rather as they do, your teen driver may replicate your actions, and you may end up having to bear the guilt of their misconduct on the road. I submit it is better to know that you have done all that you knew to do than to ponder on the "what if's." You may have to sit down and reexamine your attitude toward the traffic laws. This means you will have to confront some of those questions that never got to the forefront of your thinking:

1. Do I drive responsibly? Do I easily engage in road rage?

2. How does my child perceive my driving and thus his or her own?

3. Why do I speed?

4. Am I willing to obey the speed limit?

5. Do I trust my child or children to drive the way I drive?

6. Do I show a disdain for the traffic laws and people in authority?

7. Is my driving strongly influenced by my friends and by the driving public?

8. Are my friends passive about the dangers I may cause by the way I drive?

9. How long might my child last if I do nothing to positively influence his or her way of driving?

If your answer to any of these ten questions borders on the negative, then consider your teen driver's disposition towards driving and the traffic laws, because your driving does matter. According to the article "Excessive Speed Causing Upward Trend in Traffic Fatalities" in the September 2006 issue of *The Police Chief* magazine, Assistant Commissioner of the New Hampshire Department of Safety, Earl M. Sweeney expressed, "An entire generation of drivers grew up riding with parents who sported radar detectors on the dashboard and regarded speeding as a game of tag." Thus some researchers recommend that a good driving example should be set by adults.

I recall one Sunday I was driving to church. Along with me were a mother and her daughter. The speed limit changed from 35 mph on the residential road to 55 mph on the two interstates we traveled, and back to 35 mph. That evening when I spoke with the mother, she expressed to me, " … my daughter said, 'Mom, he didn't go over the speed limit.'" I was not aware that the child was paying attention to my driving; she looked pretty relaxed in the car and probably was observing the outside scene. Other than seeing the car's speedometer initially, how did she know I was not speeding? Perhaps she saw the multitude of vehicles that flew past me, as though I was in a time-dilation system. The bottom line is your teen driver does pay attention to the way you drive, so give them every reason to value integrity driving.

Research and New Initiatives

In addition to being a good example of integrity driving to your teen driver, you should know what researchers are finding about teen driving. We have research showing some of the same factors causing teen motor vehicle crashes. Inexperience, night driving, and risky behaviors are just a few factors contributing to the increase in teen motor vehicle crashes and fatalities.

"Per mile driven, teen drivers are more likely to be involved in a fatal crash than other drivers," said Mary Pat McKay, MD, MPH, and director of the Center for Injury Prevention and Control at the George Washington University Medical Center in Washington, DC. "The increased risk for crashing results from a combination of inexperience and immaturity, particularly a tendency toward riskier behavior"

(American College of Emergency Physicians).

The article offers parents the following advice: limit the number of passengers driven by your teen, limit nighttime driving, choose a safe vehicle, stress the importance of safety belt usage, and have a zero tolerance for alcohol use. The article also indicated that "…the majority of deaths that occur in crashes involving young drivers are to other people, particularly their own passengers." In Georgia we witnessed this fact in November 2006, when one young driver made a turn that killed him and his two teen passengers, who were not even supposed to be in his vehicle according to Georgia's Graduated Driver's License law. Relative to wearing seatbelts, the American College of Emergency Physicians article also states, "…of the teens killed as occupants in motor vehicles in 2003, only 33 percent (37 percent of drivers and 25 percent of passengers) were wearing safety belts at the time of the crash." And Dr. McKay claimed that, "Even a conservative estimate, using the lowest belt effectiveness rating of 50 percent, indicates that about 1,860 of those non-belted teenagers killed in 2003 would be alive today had they just buckled up."

Joshua's Law

In an effort to reduce, if not stop, teen motor vehicle crashes and fatalities, the Georgia General Assembly has enacted the Joshua's Law, which took effect on January 1, 2007. The inspiration behind this legislation came as a result of the fatal crash involving Joshua Brown, a sixteen-year old, whose vehicle hydroplaned on July 1, 2003. Eight days after the crash Joshua died as a result of the injuries. Joshua's father, Alan Brown, expressed, "The car is a weapon, and in inexperienced hands it can be deadly (Riley)." "Since his son's death, Brown has made it his life's mission to protect young drivers by calling for stricter driver training requirements and improving educational programs in the state of Georgia and beyond" (Riley). I saw a newscast where Mr. Brown mentioned that he does not want other parents to experience what he and his wife had to endure.

Joshua's Law mandates that a teen who seeks to obtain a driver's license before his seventeenth birthday must complete a state-approved driver's education course and forty hours of adult supervision. Six of these hours must be during the night. This law builds upon Georgia's TADRA [Teenage and Adult Driver Responsibility Act] Law, which imposes a three-stage licensing process. These laws put forth an aggressive stride by the authorities to evince the message of accountability and responsibility to our teen drivers. For instance, a high school student could have his license revoked if he has at least ten unexcused absences from school, or if he drops out of school. It is highly recommended that both parents and teen drivers or those teens who desire to obtain a driver's license check with their state DMV or Governor's Office of Highway Safety for an update of any laws pertaining to teen driving.

While the main focus of Joshua's Law is to provide adequate training for our young drivers, researchers say teen drivers are at high risk of crashing due to alcohol consumption before driving, driving with other teen passengers, and a lack of seatbelt usage.

> Having other teen passengers is another important risk factor for teen motor vehicle crashes. In General, teens are more likely than older drivers to be in crashes caused by driver error. When driving with friends in the car, teens can become distracted, causing the driver to give less adequate attention to the new task of driving and increasing the possibility of error.
>
> (Martin and Brown)

The authors also indicated that "Researchers have tried to measure the risk associated with teen passengers, with one study finding that teen drivers' crash risk rises exponentially with one, two, or three or more passengers in the car."

So Many Voices

Everyone is competing for our attention: the news media, radio stations, family, friends, and associates, to name a few. Whoever gets to rent our minds the most is certain to influence us more. Our children are bombarded daily with so many voices and they must make a conscious decision as to which voices are necessary to listen to and are profitable. In December 2006, I heard one female student say to a male student that she could not function without her phone. She expressed she had to spend one day without it and she could not talk to all of her friends. I asked her what her minutes plan was, to which she said 1500 a month. Being curious, I inquired how many of those minutes she used. She replied, "All!" I was thinking, *With 1500 minutes plus spending many hours on many peoples' favorite Web site (MySpace), how do you get anything of greater significance done?* Teen drivers interact with other teens, some of whom do not know right from wrong. They listen to so much information and must weigh the good, if any, in all of it. If parents are not setting good driving standards, both by their actions and their words, then their teen driver hears only those outside their homes, especially some of those who themselves pay no attention to driving responsibly.

The entertainment industry pumps millions of dollars a year to attract and sell products and services to children, while some gangs offer their prospects alluring reasons as to why joining the gang is in their best interest. We live in a time when public education seems to be failing and our teaching methods must be reformed and refined consistently just to keep up in attracting students to learning. If a teacher fails to improve his or her methods or even garner more knowledge and its applications, his learners will become even more difficult to reach. The bottom line is someone is always speaking to the teen driver, and so I ask, "Should it not be the parent(s) who get to influence him the most [about driving]? Our news media shows us many video clips and photos of how terrorist groups are teaching and training young children and youths to hate, the same principle taught by some parents in this country concerning racial and color prejudice. And where has it gotten us today? Teen drivers will abide by the rules once they are explained to them, once adults become good examples of obeying the rules, and once the standards are strictly enforced.

It is wonderful that there are many programs geared towards teaching teens how to drive "defensively," as well as the push for and enactment of several laws restricting the minimum driving age, and other factors that are common in teen motor vehicle crashes. All of these initiatives are necessary and beneficial. Nevertheless, many parents still do not know about many of these new initiatives. However, you cannot wait for the government to enact laws to help save your teen's life in case of a motor vehicle crash. It is good that our government is making consistent progress in developing means to curtail motor vehicle fatalities. In the effort to preserve lives, for example, the DOT has installed guardrails and other technology that increase a person's chance of surviving a motor vehicle crash. Automobile manufactures are constantly researching safety mechanisms and redesigning their vehicles so as to increase an occupant's chance of surviving a motor vehicle crash. And all of these efforts are wonderful and necessary! We must also realize that if we do not stop to reexamine our attitudes towards driving and to each other and to make a positive change, we will always have to witness the tragedy of the road, because the ultimate preventative measure is doing what is right. The guardrails do not prevent the crash, nor do the safety features of your vehicle.

Despite the warnings from the Governor's High Safety Association, the National Highway Traffic Safety Administration, the Insurance Institute of Highway Safety Association, the Police Chief, the International Association of Chief of Police, Mothers Against Drunk Driving, Partners for Highway Safety, and from some concerned parents, students, and other private organizations, many drivers continue to ignore these positive voices until tragedy strikes on our roads. But tragedy does not have to continue if we choose to value each other to the point where we submit ourselves to seeing their future brighter than ever. Then the next generation will be able to grow up in complete obedience and never have to experience what we currently see.

Teen and Young Drivers

When I was a teen, I hated corrections, because they required me to stop having fun as I had envisioned it. My father used to tell my mother, " … let Jermaine stick around … " He told her this every time he planned to send a gift home while he was at work. I hated the fact that I was still at home when he was leaving for work, because his favorite speech was sure to follow: " … let Jermaine stick around … " Then at times my parents warned me not to go out with my friends because they sensed danger was sure to follow. As for me, danger was actually a companion. I said this since I never learned from the misfortune of disobeying my parents. I either ended up in a fight, or almost drowned when I escaped to go swimming, or got stung by bees and almost bitten by dogs. The point I am making is, as a child, I could not discern right from wrong to the point of obeying my parents. As a result, I reaped the negative consequences.

And so I appeal to you, teen drivers and young adults. Whose life is riding upon your obedience? If you choose to please your friends over doing what is right behind the wheel, whose family will have to bear the consequence as a result of your decision? Who will pay the price for your decisions? Pause and really think about these questions. Throughout this book, I urge drivers to reconsider their driving habits and thus change their attitudes about driving, because one man's decision could affect an entire generation. When you choose to obey, others will benefit. You might not see it immediately, but in the end, it will be because you have chosen to do what was right!

Consider the student code of conduct booklet that schools issue to each student at the beginning of every school year. In DeKalb County, Georgia, we issue each student a copy of this booklet and make him sign for it. The signature bears witness that the student was given a copy of this booklet and was made aware of its content and the consequences for disobeying the rules and regulations therein. Yet some of these very students end up creating a panic and some of them have to ride in the backseat of a patrol car, and some of them are still in juvenile detention. Even though these students were made aware of the information and consequences in the booklet, they still committed an offense. In like manner, if you disobey the traffic laws, which were created to help preserve your life, as well as others, someone may end up six feet under the earth, if not severely injured.

However, you can begin the process of integrity driving today by simply wearing a seatbelt. I know it can be a little discomforting, but if you happen to crash, you will see the benefit of wearing one. Many teen drivers I spoke with said wearing seatbelts was "not cool." If you share this view, then check out what happens in one second of a crash. The following information was obtained from the Virginia DOT Web site (see reference #24 for Internet address.)

Here is a description of the final moment of an unbelted driver whose vehicle runs into a stationary object at 55 mph.

- **1/10 of a second**   The front bumper and grill of the car collapse. If the car has an air bag, it is already inflated.

- **2/10 of a second**   The hood crumples, rises and strikes the windshield as the rear wheels lift from the ground. The fender wraps around the struck object. The driver's legs stiffen and snap.

- **3/10 of a second**   The steering wheel starts to disintegrate and the steering column aims for the driver's chest.

- **4/10 of a second**   The car's front end is wrecked and the rear end is still moving at 35 mph. The driver's body is stilling traveling at 55 mph. In a head-on crash, an airbag gives the driver a 31% greater chance of surviving (when wearing a seatbelt). Air bags are not designed to protect drivers and passengers in rear, side and rollover crashes.

- **5/10 of a second**   If the car was not equipped with an airbag, the driver is impaled on the steering column. Blood rushes into the driver's lungs.

- **6/10 of a second**   The driver's feet are ripped out of his shoes. The brake pedal snaps off. The car's frame buckles in the middle. Without an air bag, the driver's head smashes into the windshield. The rear wheels fall back to the ground.

- **7/10 of a second**   The passenger door hinges rip loose and the rear doors fly open. The back seat breaks free and strikes the driver, who may already be dead.

It is not my intention to scare you into making the decision to obey the traffic laws, because any decision made out of fear is weak and will be compromised. Rather, I want you to see and fully understand the risk you would be taking and the pain others will have to endure if you choose to disobey what is right.

A Living Example of Integrity Driving
(An Example You Can Follow)

I write to you, America, because I believe you will change; I believe you will change your mindset towards driving and doing so with integrity. I write to you, parents and adults, because you are a beacon of light to your children, an example they can and will follow. I write to you, young adults and teen drivers, because America's great destiny is in your capable hands, and our legacy will continue through you and your children. I write to you, America, because the world is always watching us and is strongly encouraged by our firmness towards righteousness and justice, towards positive change and freedom, towards peace and safety, and towards the belief that all men are indeed created equal and that *"when the rights of one man is denied, the rights of all men are denied,"* as President John F. Kennedy once remarked.

My Early Years of Driving

I have been driving for nearly thirteen years, and I have witnessed both bad and good driving; myself having experienced the bad, I now am delighted to do the good. I once received an email in my college years entitled "What I Have Learned." In it the sender listed one thing that individuals from ages ranging from three to eighty-something said they have learned. One person said, "I have learned that no matter where I go the world's worst drivers have followed me there." To this I concurred, because I was once one of those drivers.

There were times when I drove and had to stop at red lights. I never liked to stop, so I made a right turn, drove across the road into the gas station on the other side of the light, and then continued on my way. I became so good at this I began to laugh at those who got caught at the light, priding myself as a skillful and smart driver, until I discovered that the cops would take pleasure in writing you a nice ticket for dangerous driving. Think about it, that is not how the road was designed, but I made my own road as I traveled.

Furthermore, I used to blaze the outermost lane on the interstates and freeways (the so-called "fast lane") all the way just before the exit at which I would get off then cut across all lanes of traffic to the right lane just to make the exit. I was very good at this; it boosted my adrenaline! Even when I had passengers, I practiced my way of driving. If they wanted to ride with me, it had to be my way or no way, and if they did not like it, then they needed their own transportation. With this mindset it was easy for me to tailgate. I flew down those interstates, from Georgia to Alabama, and from Georgia through both Carolinas, Virginia, Maryland, all the way to New York. When I came upon drivers who caused me to slow my speed, I first flashed my high-beam headlight. When that did not work, I sped up just under their bumper, and when that did not work, I gave them the horn. The bright light worked most of the time. But when nothing worked, I passed them with moderate speeds so they could see my face to know that I did not appreciate their refusal to "Get out of the way!"

In addition, driving during my college years was wild! Many days I went to bed late, got up late, and procrastinated for a while, before leaving for school. Since classes were in downtown Atlanta, I decided that the only way to get to class, some twenty miles away, was to hit the I-20 and fly down that joint! With no cops in view, I floored the accelerator for as long as I could. I strongly believed I would never crash. Then traffic backed up. With class starting in five minutes and being stuck in traffic nearly one exit away, I pulled over into the emergency lane with joy, knowing the other drivers were not as smart and bold as I was. I got away with it. So I continued to practice it for a while. And guess what? Despite my speed and dangerous and reckless driving, I never made it to class early or on time.

Wasted Dollars

In mathematics, two negative numbers multiplied together make a positive number, yet I have never witnessed this phenomenon when driving. In fact, two negatives result in a higher insurance premium. And that was exactly what I got for speeding, and speeding, and yet speeding again.

The North Carolina Violation

The real big tickets started in November 2002 when I was returning home from Maryland for the Thanksgiving holidays. Riding with me was one of my cousins, who was also eager to get out of Georgia for the holidays. This was my first trip driving myself out of state. I was really looking forward to seeing many sites. Before I left Maryland to return to Georgia, my brother warned me not to speed, especially in Virginia and North Carolina. He knew why because he was used to getting a few tickets when he visited us, both coming and going.

Well, I heard him, but I did not obey. I had just bought my new car and was determined to know how many miles I could get per tank. So I drove on E (empty signal) for a long while. There were no cops on patrol in Virginia (at least this was what I thought since I did not see any,) so I was doing 90 mph. Hey, I was on an 11-hour drive if I had obeyed the speed limit, but that was time I could afford. I got out of Virginia and into North Carolina like Speedy Gonzales, (a name my grandfather used to describe someone who moved really fast.) I was cutting the air, blazing the trail, only to realize I needed gas. I got off at an exit for gas, but the station was closed. So I got back on the interstate (I-95) doing 80 mph, not realizing that the faster I drove the faster the fuel was burning up. Every driver was in the inner lane, but Speedy had to trail blaze the outer lane. Those blue lights went on the moment I flew pass an unmarked patrol car. Before this moment, my cousin in the car with me was warning me, "Jermaine, slow down…remember what your brother told you?" Also, my brother called periodically to determine my location and to inquire if everything was well. He once asked, "You're not speeding?" When Trooper T.D. Kato walked up to my car, my cousin began laughing at the fact I got caught. I wanted to kick him out!

That ticket cost me $450. I was doing 80 mph in a 55 mph work zone, a sure reason for a double fine. Christmas was coming and I had other plans for that money. I got back to Georgia with an outrage against the entire state of North Carolina. I had even planned to take my case to the media, being indignant about the whole situation and listening to the wrong folks encouraging me to do so. But I calmed down and paid the ticket; I even had to get a lawyer to go to court, because that kind of ticket required a court appearance, no exception!

The Georgia Violation

Shortly after this North Carolina incident I was again doing what I was known for: speeding. This time I was on Interstate 20 near downtown Atlanta. I was running late for a service held at World Changers Church International in College Park, Georgia. I wanted to see and hear the Godfather of Faith, Dr. Frederick K.C. Price speak. The service began around 7:00 p.m., but I left home, some one hour away, near 7:00 p.m. Blazing down I-20, I banked a wide turn in the lane just before the HOV (High Occupancy Vehicle) lane and saw a trooper jump into his car parked in the emergency lane after the HOV. It was too late to slow down; his radar gun locked me in at 80 mph. When the trooper came to my car, he announced I was doing 80 mph on a 55 mph stretch. He asked, "Where are you going?" I told him that I was going to World Changers to hear Dr. Price speak. He inquired, "Who is he?" With joy, I responded, "He is a pastor and teacher from Los Angeles, California." I thought this was a good enough excuse to get off with a warning, but he ticketed me anyway. He wrote the ticket and told me to slow down. I was furious! There I was, going to *church* and this trooper had the nerve to give me a ticket! I thought long and hard on the fact that I got a ticket on my way to church. Oh, I was so angry! But when I really considered my actions, I rescinded because the person I was going to hear speak was a man whose lifestyle was full of integrity, and there I was practicing the opposite. I ended up paying $102.00 upfront money for my disobedience. Upfront money is what you pay for the ticket; the backend money is what the insurance companies would impose for having points on your license.

The West Virginia Violation

Oh, there goes Speedy Gonzales for the third time, doing what he does best, speeding—on I-77 through West Virginia heading for

New York. This time I was enjoying a summer break and was driving some New Yorkers home. A novice to speeding tricks, I entered the far left lane doing 80 mph. The speed limit? Oh, you should know by now. There are multiple internet books that teach you how to speed and not get caught, with tricks such as the "Rabbit Trap," but Speedy was not aware of them. So I was flying past all types of vehicles, from small cars to light trucks, from eighteen wheelers to tour buses. But the trooper this time was parked parallel to the interstate in one of those crossover paths on the divided interstate (separated by grass and trees.) When I saw him, he was gearing up to hit the interstate. So I slowed down after passing, but it was too late, the gun had already read my speed. This was my third ticket, costing just under $180. But I was not angry this time, although it was an inconvenience.

The Repeated Georgia Violation

When would Speedy learn his lesson? You would think three tickets would do the job of getting me to obey the traffic laws. It was like a dog returning to his own vomit. Even though I disliked paying the state my well-earned money for traffic violations, my actions did very little to substantiate my dislike. This time I was returning from Sparta, Georgia, from a friend's. The speed limit was 70 mph for a very long distance on I-20 west, so my mind was acclimated to this pace. When the speed limit changed to 55 mph in Newton County, Speedy increased his speed by 10 mph. As I banked a wide turn, I spotted a Newton sheriff car, parked perpendicular to the interstate. The sheriff slowly merged unto the interstate and began pursuit of me. The feeling I got this time was frightening! I thought my license was going to be revoked, because this was my forth speeding violation in under a year and a half. I pleaded with the sheriff, "Sir, I just got a ticket, and I really cannot afford another." He took my license and insurance card to his vehicle. I looked through the rearview mirror and noticed him talking on his radio. When he returned, he said, "I will give you a warning this time ... " That was all I needed to hear. When I thought I could not do 55 mph, I was convinced that it was possible, at least for the rest of the trip home. This was my last speeding ticket. To this day, no officer can charge me for speeding, even if they secretly place a tracker on my vehicles, because I am ID (well-acquainted with Integrity Driving.)

Mental Reprogramming

Change must be preceded by actions corresponding to a different thought. Doing the same thing and expecting a different result is insane. I had to learn this concerning my driving. They say that God is always speaking. Well, when I heard him for the first time about my driving, I obeyed for a short while, but getting those tickets with a gigantic price tag, really amplified His voice. I made a promise to Him, "I will never speed again." Of course, I was talking about deliberately speeding, like knowing you are late, so you will speed just this last time. No, I stopped!

I once read an excerpt from Dr. Frederick K.C. Price's book, *Integrity: The Guarantee For Success*. Dr. Price expressed,

> America has become a nation of lawbreakers. We make up our own laws as we go along. Somewhere along the line, we decided that a stop sign means to slow down. If you were to ask someone why they failed to stop at a stop sign, they would probably say, "But everyone does rolling stops. The majority rules, despite what the law says; and any and everything is now considered to be all right until someone gets hurt ...

I enjoyed the excerpt so much that I purchased the book. On page 38, Dr. Price mentions, "Until you are able to stand up for what you believe is right—regardless of what others think—your feelings will always affect your ability to properly discern right from wrong," and so on this principle I want to encourage you to reconsider your position about driving with integrity.

Drivers speed because of many reasons, such as running late for work, trying to get to the store before closing time, because it pumps up their adrenaline, or because it is comfortable to them. People speed and do all other kinds of illegal activities while driving to make up for convenience. They do these things so often that their initial thoughts about them became an action, which become habit, which forms their character, and ultimately determines their destiny. When I realized these things, I decided I would do my best to obey the traffic laws. I refrained from speeding because I really did not want to, or like, getting speeding tickets or any other tickets for that matter. I must admit, it took a lot of energy and effort to do right because my mind was fixed on driving dangerously.

So the question I asked myself was, *Am I willing to obey the speed limit?* After I answered this question with a convincing yes, my next question was, *How will I do it; what will it cost me?* I realized that my way of thinking had to change, which was exactly what I began to do. I was so convinced about driving responsibly and at the speed limit that I changed my insurance policy from full coverage to liability. My insurance agent at the time informed me that changing to liability coverage will not cover property damage to me if I cause a crash. However, I could take liability coverage with the option of paying a premium to protect against property damage to me should the other driver not have insurance. So I purchased the latter package. I changed to liability because I was convinced I would not be the cause of a crash. I truly believed I could drive the speed limit, observe my surroundings, drive defensively, and obey the traffic laws to the extent of my knowledge. My mind was converted to being obedient to the traffic laws. I began making my confessions: "I will never speed again!" "I will drive responsibly." "I will never crash again!" Believe me, to this day, I joyfully can say that my decision to obey the traffic laws has not been in vain. I became conscious of the great labor our men and women in law enforcement are contributing to this great nation. Similarly, by driving with integrity I have developed a road block in my mind against knowingly and willfully violating the traffic laws.

Had I not counted the cost for my obedience to the traffic laws, I would have reverted to my predisposition when driving. The temptations to breaking the laws were constant. But my commitment to integrity driving has kept me from falling victim to all of them. I remember when I began driving the speed limit there were multiple cars with some very attractive young women passing by me. I really wanted to catch up, but my commitment kept running across my mind and would not permit me to speed. Then I was running late for work for many consecutive days, but my commitment to driving with integrity became stronger and stronger as I continued to practice it, and today my commitment enables me to write to you about this marvelous and proven lifestyle that will ensure your safety, as well as others,' your financial profit, and many other benefits to you and everyone around you. One of these benefits is better gas mileage. When I used to drive without integrity, I was getting 330 miles per tank. But now that I am driving with integrity, I am getting around 530 miles, and sometimes more.

Let me show you what a strong mental disposition integrity driving is and how you can never lose when you practice it. To show you what I am talking about I will use an illustration of the pig.

> Say you found a small strayed pig in the mud. Looking at him was unbearable because he was completely covered in filth; even portions of his eyeballs were muddy. So you decided to take him in as your pet. You cleaned him up nicely by shampooing and giving him a thorough bath. After bathing him, you sprayed

some sweet smelling fragrance on him, put a nice piggy suit on him and hugged him ecstatically for a good ten seconds! Then the phone rang. You placed sweet piggy on the couch and went to answer the phone. After ten minutes you returned to your new found joy, only to discover he was gone. With haste you exited the room and found piggy outside in the mud, worse than he was when you first saw him. Now instead of road rage, you begin to develop pig rage.

Why did piggy go back to the mud?

In case you did not know, piggy's mental was the same after the shampooing, the bath, and the sweet fragrance, as it was before. The bath, the sweet fragrance, and the clothes were all external remedies to piggy's problem. All piggy knew was playing in the mud again. To keep piggy from the mud, a new mental program was needed. And this is the principle behind integrity driving. It changes your former attitude towards driving. Hence, you do not have to run to court with tricks and the hopes that the officer who wrote you the ticket will not show up. Integrity driving distills the idea of ever having to go before a judge for something that you were well aware of; it sets up a wall of protection around you. Unlike the person who gets advice from some sources that promise to teach you how to speed and not get caught, integrity driving promises you how to drive in obedience to the traffic laws and reap tremendous benefits when doing so. It is far better than having to learn new tricks on how to evade the radar gun and how to scan for cops before making that illegal turn.

Why spend so much energy in scheming your way down the road when you do not have to? Why be found guilty of vehicular man-slaughter when you can drive responsibly? Why get a ticket for speeding when you do not have to speed? I remember one guy placed on his Web site that he got pulled over for speeding seventeen times, got four tickets, beat three of them, and the one he was convicted of was due to his inexperience in manipulating and abusing the law. He was very proud to share his so-called "wisdom," and he believed he was providing a valuable service. Now I am not knocking him, but I am rather dealing with principles. We spend millions of dollars annually to research causes of motor vehicle crashes and safety features. Well, there goes our answer. Some drivers do as they please. Consequently, their children see their complete disregard for law and order, and thus they take the path of least resistance, even though many of those paths lead to pain and grief in the end.

But integrity driving is like a huge umbrella of protection against the negative vicissitudes of driving. Just as an umbrella does not stop the rain from falling, but stops it from getting on you, so integrity driving will not prevent the cops from parking in inconspicuous locations along the interstates or any other type of roads and clocking your speed, but it prevents them from legally giving you a ticket. It will not prevent the circumstances from coming at you, but it prevents them from having a negative impact on your driving.

On December 30, 2006, for instance, I was driving on I-20 East by night, around 10:40 p.m., when suddenly a car flew past all the cars in my vicinity, doing more than the 65 mph limit. I flashed my high-beam headlight to warn the driver to slow down. He completely ignored the warning. What he did not know was the dark patrol car parked perpendicular to the interstate, inconspicuous at far distances. I saw the patrol car back up and begin pursuit of the speeder. I imagined him saying, "Man, somebody was just flashing his lights to warn me!" Although this speeder did not respect me, he respected that light and probably was very upset about getting a ticket. This is exactly what I mean by saying integrity driving will prevent the officer from giving you a ticket. I was on the same road with this driver who was speeding. But I chose to obey the law while he disobeyed, and it cost him.

Integrity driving eliminates all probability of having to deal with posthumous motor vehicle crashes, as well as knowingly committing any traffic violation. Some drivers say, "This is my last time speeding; I will stop after this trip." Well, think about it like this: waiting for the rain to fall before you purchase an umbrella is ridiculous. The best time to purchase an umbrella is before the rain comes. Hence, the best time to commit to integrity driving is right now, not when the officer is behind you with his siren on. I took early retirement from dangerous driving. Today, I am enjoying the fruit of my decision, and so I encourage you to do the same.

So you may ask, "How can I avoid speeding tickets and all the other traffic violations?" The only sure answer I have found, the lifestyle that works to everyone's advantage, is by committing to driving with integrity. Here are some of those benefits you will experience when you do: you will

1. learn the value of time

2. save tremendous money on gasoline

3. drastically reduce the effects of wear and tear on your vehicle(s)

4. develop positive character traits

5. understand and practice honoring our men and women in law enforcement

6. escape the horrors, grief, and pain that result from crashing

7. learn to love others by your actions and not merely by your words

8. set yourself above the circumstances that exist on the roads

9. influence others in a positive way and be respected by those who value your integrity

10. prolong the days of your life

11. save yourself from having any entanglement with the law in regards to driving

12. have and maintain such a peace about driving that even road rage will have no place in you, ever

And the list continues...

The Wisdom of Integrity Driving

If you truly desire to become a person of integrity in your driving, then you will have to pinpoint "the reasons" as to why you fail to obey the laws. Remember, things just do not happen. Everything happens as a result of something that preceded it. Let us examine some scenarios to identify the underlying reasons of failing to observe the traffic laws and to driving with integrity.

Scenario 1: School Bus Scenario

Bill is on his way to work. The traffic is normal; Bill's job is thirty minutes away and his current position will put him within three minutes of arriving early. Well, somewhere along the route a school bus stops to board some students. The bus driver turns on the red lights so that the students may safely cross the street. Bill is in front of traffic, waiting for the bus to pull off. While Bill is throwing a tantrum because this stop will make him late, little Johnny, one of the students crossing the street to board the bus, remembers his backpack on the ground where all the students were standing. He turns around and slowly walks back for his bag. Bill is now in kill mode because Johnny is moving like an ant. Bill honks his horn three times within two seconds. Johnny stops to notice him, and then slowly continues and retrieves his backpack and again takes his time towards the bus. Bill is revving his engine. As Johnny boards the bus, Bill rushes past, while the bus' red safety light is still on. There goes

Officer Cooper parked in front of a subdivision while being blocked from Bill's view by the bus. Officer Cooper motions for Bill to pull over. Bill is totally furious!

Other than ignoring the bus's red light, what was Bill's problem? Why was Bill angry at Johnny? Why was Bill angry at the fact the school bus stopped? Here is the problem: Bill's target time for being at work was the same as the job's description time for him being there. If you have to be at work for 8:00 a.m. and you decide to get there at 8:00 a.m., then you may experience Bill's frustration and disappointment. Instead, Bill should have decided to be at work about thirty minutes early, which would have required him to do some preparation the night before. His lack of preparation or whatever that may have caused him to leave at the time he left resulted in road rage, being ticketed for running a school bus' red safety light, and actually being late for work (and may lose pay depending upon his job.)

Scenario 2: Traffic Jam Scenario

It's the event no driver likes—a traffic jam—and Susie has to deal with it today. Susie's favorite television show is about to begin in fifteen minutes, but at the rate traffic is moving she will miss ten minutes of it by the time she gets home. She quarrels with herself in the car while the people who caused the hold up are debating as to who caused the crash, Susie remembers passing a back road less than a quarter mile before. She has to make a decision. Cars are moving rapidly and constantly in the opposite direction. If Susie makes a left turn into a driveway then comes back out to go in the opposite direction, she may have to wait until the road is clear to do so, which will take a while. Instead, she makes a forbidden U-turn and ends up causing a speeder to run into her rear bumper. Forget about her favorite show: she will be there for a long time.

Could Susie have avoided this crash? What was her problem? If you said impatience you are absolutely correct. Some drivers will trade patience in a second just to get to where they want to go, even if their decision bears grave consequences. Do we not see it all the time? People run the red light because they do not want to wait for it to change. Some get away with it, but others are not as fortunate. Susie probably thought no one noticed her actions, but she miscalculated. Although the other driver was speeding, Susie will get a ticket, because she has also violated the law. Do you see how integrity driving is like an umbrella to keep trouble from ever making it to you? The decision to commit to driving with integrity is yours to make. You can practice driving like Bill and Susie, or you can choose to drive with integrity by obeying all the traffic laws. And look at this—Susie probably would not have made the illegal U-turn if one or both of those drivers who had caused the huge back up in the first place had done what was right. The lives of Susie and the speeder did depend upon the obedience of the driver(s) who caused the initial crash.

Understanding the reasons why you fail to obey the traffic laws and renewing your mind to obey these laws will develop your integrity in driving. By practicing this principle you will eventually discover the wisdom of driving with integrity, wisdom that will set you beyond the circumstances that exist on the roads daily. Others will be able to see you as a positive role model on the roads and imitate your good driving behavior. In fact, your integrity in driving will be "…like the fixed stars that shine so unchanged that the sailor may depend upon them to steer his course (Clason 13)." And so I ask, why learn tricks on how to speed and commit other traffic violations and probably get caught one day when you can master obeying the traffic laws and never have to get entangled with the law or an officer? In the classroom, for instance, it really amazes me how a student could spend so much time preparing to cheat on a test only to get caught, when that same time could have been spent studying the material. The wisdom gained from practicing driving with integrity will guarantee you a richer experience when you drive and others will greatly benefit from your obedience.

Like The Sun

Integrity driving is like the sun that daily completes its circuit. All of my life, I have never seen the sun rise from the west and set in the east, or rise from the north and set in the south, or rise from the south and set in the north. Instead, the sun rises from the east and sets in the west. We see its light everyday, and no one really pauses to see if the sun is shining so he may go about his business. We expect everyday for the sun to do what it was created to do. Its energy and light are necessary and beneficial to every living thing and every living person's survival on this planet. In like manner, when you practice driving with integrity, others will be able to rely on your obedience. They will not have to question whether you are a safe driver, or whether you are driving with insurance. Just as the sun rises from the east and sets in the west, you will keep the traffic laws without deviating. Just as the sun is necessary for our survival, so will your obedience to the traffic laws be necessary for others' survival on the road. Your good driving habit will be unquestionable and consistent. It will be like Mr. Clason said, "… the sun that shines today is the sun that shone when thy father was born, and will still be shining when thy last grandchild shall pass into the darkness."

Because It Is the Right Thing to Do

When you practice driving with integrity, you make it almost impossible for you to disobey what is right. In fact, when the thought of disobeying what you know or believe to be right pops up, every fiber of your being will begin to remind you of your commitment and will empower you to do what is right. So do not worry about the speeders and the reckless and aggressive drivers, and the other drivers violating the traffic laws and getting away with it. You have the advantage because you know better. Others' disobedience should not convince or coerce you to drive in opposition to the traffic laws. Drive right because it is the right thing to do. In the end, everyone, including yourself, will benefit from your good driving. If you have to move out of the "fast lane" so a speeder may continue in his disobedience, then in the effort to save another life, do so, and do not take it personally or let his disobedience throw you into a road rage. I had to learn this. I used to do the speed limit in the "fast lane" until I realized that some drivers will run you over if they feel like it. So I travel in the inner lanes, and still some of them get mad at me and pass from the emergency lane. This is dangerous! In fact, it became so prevalent in the state of Georgia that it compelled DOT officials to warn the driving public by displaying "Unlawful to travel on shoulders. Emergency use only" warnings on the information display screens.

Wisdom dictates you drive with integrity, and do not permit those who drive contrary to the traffic laws to upset you. Keep your peace of mind. They just do not understand the magnitude of their decisions and the way they drive. They will continue to do what they do because no one says anything to them, and because they get away with it—until someone gets hurt.

A Decision to Be Made

Are you ready to enjoy life on the roads to the fullest? Commit to integrity driving. By doing so you will be able to reach your destiny, fulfill your purpose in life, and enable others to achieve theirs as well. The truth that you were born to succeed will begin to manifest and others will see that you are important! I write to you because I believe that you will do what is right.

References

1. U.S. D.OT. NHTSA. "Transportation Secretary Mineta Calls Highway Fatalities an Epidemic, Nation Should Prevent Traffic Deaths Like Any Other Disease." Internet. Available: http://www.dot.gov/affairs/nhtsa0905.htm   Jun. 2005.

2. Governors Highway Safety Association. *Survey of The States: Speeding.* Internet. Available:http://www.ghsa.org/html/publications/pdf/surveystates2005/surveystates_speeding.pdf Jun. 2005.

3. "National Forum on Speeding: Strategies for Reducing Speeding-Related Fatalities & Injuries." Internet. Available: http://www.nhtsa.dot.gov/people/injury/enforce/NatForum-Speeding/index.htm 25 Mar. 2007.

4. U.S. D.O.T. NHTSA NCSA. *Traffic Safety Facts* 2004*: A Compilation of Motor Vehicle Crash Data from the Fatality Analysis Reporting System and the General Estimates System.* Internet. Available: http://www-nrd.nhtsa.dot.gov/pdf/nrd-30/NCSA/TSFAnn/TSF2004.pdf Jun. 2006.

   * Address to *Traffic Safety Facts* 2005*: A Compilation of Motor Vehicle Crash Data from the Fatality Analysis Reporting System*

and the General Estimates System. Internet. Available: http://www-nrd.nhtsa.dot.gov/Pubs/TSF2005.PDF 25 Apr. 2007

5. NYS DMV, Governor's Traffic Safety Committee, Office of Internet Services. "Child Safety Seats." Internet. Available: http://www.nysgtsc.state.ny.us/seat-ndx.htm Jan. 2007.

6. O'Donnell, Jayne. "Deadly teen auto crashes show a pattern." USA Today. Internet. Available: http://www.usatoday.com/money/autos/2005–0228-teen-drive-cover-usat_x.html 25 Mar. 2006.

7. National Highway Traffic Safety Administration. "Traffic Safety Facts 2004: Alcohol." DOT 809 905. Internet. Available: http://www-nrd.nhtsa.dot.gov/pdf/nrd-30/NCSA/TSF2004/809905.pdf June 2006.

8. "Why do we speed? Because we think we have a good excuse." USA Today. Internet. Available: http://www.usatoday/news/nation/2004–02–23-speed2_x.htm 25 Mar. 2006.
Similar articles may be obtained by typing the numbers 1 through 5 in place of the "2" following the word "speed."

9. FARS. "Fatality Analysis Reporting System (FARS) Web-Based Encyclopedia: Did You Know?" Internet. Available: http://www-fars.nhtsa.dot.gov/new_tips.cfm?stateid=0&year=2005&tipscat=crashes

http://www-fars.nhtsa.dot.gov/new_tips.cfm?stateid=0&year=2005&tipscat=people

http://www-fars.nhtsa.dot.gov/new_tips.cfm?stateid=0&year=2005&tipscat=children

http://www-fars.nhtsa.dot.gov/new_tips.cfm?stateid=0&year=2005&tipscat=pedestrians

http://www-fars.nhtsa.dot.gov/new_tips.cfm?stateid=0&year=2005&tipscat=vehicles

2005.

10. PBS. "The Presidents-John F. Kennedy, 35th President: Civil Rights Announcement" (2006): Internet. Available: http://www.pbs.org/wgbh/amex/presidents/35_kennedy/psources/ps_civilrights.html 7 Dec. 2006.

11. "Welcome to Brooklyn Car Accidents.com" Internet. Available: http://www.brooklyncaraccidents.com 11 Sept. 2006.

12. U.S. DOT. "Dot Releases Preliminary Estimates Of 2002 Highway Fatalities." Internet. Available: http://www.dot.gov/affairs/nhtsa1303.htm 21 Jul. 2006.

13. Gregory, Ted and McCormick, John. "Keeping teens drivers alive: What can be done to fight the No. 1 cause of death among American youths?" *Chicago Tribune* 5 Mar. 2006. Internet. Available: http://www.chicagotribune.com/news/specials/chi-060305teens-story,0,4157691.story 7 July 2006.

14. Heath, Brad. "Dangerous drives kill hundreds in Michigan." *Detroit News* 30 Mar. 2003. Internet. Available: http://www.detnews.com/2003/specialreport/0303/30/a01-122390.htm 26 Mar. 2007.

15. U.S. DOT Federal Highway Administration. "Intersections" Internet. Available: http://safety.fhwa.dot.gov/intersections/index.htm 8 Jan. 2007.

16. "One Crash Every 2.8 Minutes: Cobb leads metro area in perilous intersections." *Atlanta-Journal Constitution* 21 Oct. 2006: A1.

17. *World's Deadliest Plane Crash.* Dir. Chantal Hébert. NOVA, 2006.

18. FARS. "Fatality Analysis Reporting System (FARS) Web-Based Encyclopedia: National Statistics." Internet. Available: http://www-fars.nhtsa.dot.gov 27 Mar. 2006.

19. Price, D.D., Frederick K.C. *Integrity: The Guarantee for Success* Los Angeles: Faith One Publishing, 2000.

20. Sweeney, Earl M. "Excessive Speed Causing Upward Trend in Traffic Fatalities." *The Police Chief* Sept. 2006. Internet. Available: http://policechiefmagazine.org/magazine/index.cfm?useaction=display_arch&article_id=1001&issue_id=92006 26 Mar. 2007.

21. American College of Emergency Physicians. "Emergency Physicians Offer Advice on Decreasing Teen Motor Vehicle Fatalities." Internet. Available: http://acep.org/webportal/Newsroom/NR/general/2005/080105.html 24 Nov. 2006.

22. Riley, Ricky. "License to Drive." *VOX: Voice of A Generation* Oct. 2006: Page 12.

23. Martin, Pilar S., Brown, Ph.D, Brett V. "Are Teens Driving Safer?" Internet. Available: http://www.childtrendsdatabank.org/PDF/teen%20driving.pdf 24 Nov. 2006.

24. VDOT. *Adventures In Driving: Survive the Ride!* Internet. Available:http://www.vdot.virginia.gov/info/resources/AID-booklet.pdf 26 Mar. 2007.

25. Clason, George S. *The Richest Man In Babylon.* New York: Signet, 1988.